DISTINCTLY WELCOMING

Christian presence in a multifaith society

DISTINCTLY WELCOMING

Christian presence in a

multifaith society

Richard Sudworth

Scripture Union, 207-209 Queensway, Bletchley, MK2 2EB, England, UK
Email: info@scriptureunion.org.uk
Website: www.scriptureunion.org.uk

© 2007 by Richard Sudworth

ISBN: 978 1 84427 317 1

Scripture Union Australia
Locked Bag 2, Central Coast Business Centre, NSW 2252
www.su.org.au

First published in the U.K. by Scripture Union, 2007

British Library Cataloguing-in-Publication data
A catalogue record for this book is available from the British Library.

Cover design: David Lund Design

Internal design and typesetting by Servis Filmsetting Ltd, Manchester

Printed in Great Britain by Creative Print and Design, Ebbw Vale, Wales

Scripture Union is an international Christian charity working with churches in
more than 130 countries, providing resources to bring the good news about Jesus
Christ to children, young people and families and to encourage them to develop
spiritually through the Bible and prayer. As well as our network of volunteers, staff
and associates who run holidays, church-based events and school Christian groups,
we produce a wide range of publications and support those who use our resources
through training programmes.

To share in further discussion of issues raised by this book and to see the author's
reflections on news events relating to our multi-faith world, go to the blog,
www.distinctlywelcoming.com

With love to my fellow-travellers
in this diverse world:
Fiona, Nellie and Dylan

Endorsements

'Being a Christian amongst people of others faiths is so fundamental, so essential a thing in 21st Century Europe that you'd
think we'd have all spent many hours thinking about it. But we
haven't – most of us have given little or no thought to this hugely
significant aspect of our life and mission, and our responses are
cobbled together from equal measures of fear, ignorance and self-
righteousness. Not so Richard Sudworth.

Richard is passionate, articulate, biblical and determined, and
he brings to his subject the considerable fruit of many years of
patient practice. This is a lively and well-paced book, avoided the
pitfalls of "dull worthiness" so often associated with inter-faith
dialogue. Reading it will bring rich rewards for the church worker
or missionary in a multi-faith context; for the youth worker in any
contemporary urban context, or just for the concerned Christian
who wants to live in the real world that actually surrounds us
rather than the fantasy created by an out-of-date and out-of-touch
church. If you live in the 19th Century you probably won't need to
read this book. If you live in the 21st, you must'.

Gerard Kelly (Crossroads International Church, Amsterdam)

'I am really excited about this book. How we as Christians relate
to other faiths and cultures is one of the two big mission challenges
we face (along with the care of the creation). This book reframes
the debate in a way that takes it out of the old arguments and
domains and opens it up in fresh ways. Richard's passion and
wisdom shine through and I hope his dream comes true that a new
generation will engage in the debate and take up the challenge'.

Jonny Baker (Church Mission Society)

'An accessible and thought-provoking introduction to one of the crucial questions facing Christians in a plural post-Christendom culture – how to move beyond assumptions, fears and stereotypes to engage graciously, hopefully and sensitively with members of other faith communities. Combining cultural analysis, mission theology, biblical reflection, stories and practical application, this book encourages us to celebrate the diversity of our emerging culture, discover God at work in unexpected places and share our faith in the context of friendship and mutual respect'.

Stuart Murray Williams (Urban Expression)

Contents

Acknowledgements

Many thanks to:

Andrew Smith, aka Smeeee, for providing the material on Youth and Children's ministry in Chapter 6, 'Young at Heart'.

Joy Madeiros, for the foreword and her work on Chapter 3, 'Distinctive Faith'.

Kumar Rajagopalan, for permitting reproduction of his story and the provision of his material in Chapter 8, 'Bringing it all Back Home', on an inclusive church.

Thanks also to:

Ann Bower, Gill Marchant, Robin Thomson, Nigel Pimlott, Martin Thomas and Jonny Baker for comments, suggestions and constructive critiques.

Toby Howarth, Pall Singh, Paul Francis, Smeeee, Richard Woods and Paul Bendor-Samuel for inspiration, encouragement, mentoring and friendship. This book is but the smallest fruit of your investment and vision in my life.

www.distinctlywelcoming.com

Foreword

by Joy Madeiros

Britain, whose Head of State appoints the Archbishop of Canterbury and whose Bishops sit in the House of Lords, is slowly waking up to what it means to have an increasingly multi-faith identity. On the one hand, it welcomes its new image. From what we are led to believe, the face of multicultural Britain made all the difference to the successful Olympics bid. However, the confusion about whether crosses or veils can or should be worn and the endless discussion about what it means to be British indicate that the nation is not as much at ease with its identity as some glossy presentations would have you believe.

But it's not all bad news. Over the last few years, Government has successfully encouraged faith groups and communities to come to the table as equal partners in community regeneration and development. It has also introduced religious discrimination regulations to protect people in employment; the Equality Act outlaws discrimination on the grounds of religion and belief in the delivery of goods and services and legislation also exists to protect people from victimisation based on religious and racial hatred. The diversity agenda now firmly recognises religion and belief as a difference in terms of identity, along with other categories of difference such as race, age, gender, disability and sexual orientation and, for the first time in the UK, there is an officially recognised body – the Commission for Equality and Human Rights – that has responsibility for advising on matters relating to discrimination on the grounds of religion and belief.

However, while the public is learning to respect religious rights at the level of dress, food, prayer times and holy days, and recognises that Government should ensure faith communities are engaged as partners, many faith groups and people of faith still encounter suspicion, prejudice or religious ignorance.

It would seem that, while the existence and even the activities of faith groups are acceptable, the faith of faith groups is still very problematic.

Is this, perhaps, because a large portion of the British public now have no experience of religion for themselves, and do not know what it means to have a faith motivation or how to relate to it? Not so long ago, even if you had rejected faith for yourself, it was more than likely that you would have grown up in a churchgoing family or had a relationship with a family member who ensured that you went along to a place of worship. But this kind of experience is far less common today.

Or is it because the battle for 'secularism' has been won hands down? The role of the Church has receded significantly by comparison to what it was two or three centuries ago and religion has become essentially a private matter. Church has been relegated by the media to an army of 'do-gooders' who are willing but not very relevant and, worse still, often not very professional. Alastair Campbell, No 10's famous one–time communications guru, will only ever be remembered for telling the nation that 'we don't do God'. So, despite the increased interest in spirituality and the significant changes in the faith landscape, the Church appears to have colluded with its own demise and as a result, the UK has grown pretty reluctant to acknowledge its rôle in society. While the media are desperate to hear Tony Blair say that he prays with George Bush or that he prays at all, 'secularism' has capitalised on the fact that the Church has left itself behind, along with its ability to prove its credibility in the public square.

Or is it because people believe what they read in the press and have come to the conclusion that religion belongs to the fanatics who are capable of creating chaos and disaster?

Or, finally, is it perhaps more to do with the fact that Christianity in the UK, having for centuries been the state religion, has never really had to explain itself and finds itself lacking confidence in its identity at a time in history when it needs more than ever to set out what it stands for?

Whatever the reason, and it's probably a mixture of all the above and more, the reality as we know it could not be more different. Beneath the headlines of religious intolerance and the experience of fear and suspicion and prejudice are the untold stories of countless individuals who, motivated by their personal faith, choose to work for the betterment of our society.

For them, faith is always personal but never private.

Like the countless politicians who have allowed their beliefs to inspire action, making a positive difference to those around them, they dedicate themselves to working for the public good.

Like the thousands of churches and other faith groups up and down the country that commit to improving the lives of society's most vulnerable, they run hostels for the homeless, alcohol recovery programmes and youth mentoring schemes in response to the needs they see around them.

Without 'public' faith, there would not have been a civil rights movement in the US or the 'Jubilee Debt Cancellation' or the 'Make Poverty History' campaigns in the UK. All these movements were inspired and led by people of faith who decided that what they believed about God and humanity should impact the world around them.

Today, the impact of 'public faith' can be seen in the vitality of the British economy. Studies have shown that faith groups contribute enormously to local economies through providing skills training, education and local service provision – very often on a voluntary basis. What would happen if their faith remained private? The economy, together with social capital, community regeneration and civic society to name but a few of the buzz words, would undoubtedly suffer.

It's true, for both right and wrong reasons, that Britain is in the grip of a fearful and, to some extent, knee-jerk reaction to faith. As people of faith, we long for Government and the public at large to recognise the extent to which faith is an essential part of everyday public life. But as the Chinese saying goes, when we point a finger of responsibility at someone else, three fingers point back at us. . . It's time for Christians to come to terms with the fact that the UK is now a multi-faith nation in which there is a plurality of religious beliefs. As much as we rightly call on Government to lever political will on our behalf, it's surely, first and foremost, our responsibility as Christians to work out how to behave in relationships with people of other faiths and how to work together in community for the good of all.

It's true to say that any time in history is unique. But this moment, the beginning of the third millennium, truly presents unique opportunities which will not come our way again. Never before have so many different faith communities found their home in the UK. Never before has Government made such an effort to bring faith groups to the partnership table. Never before has there been such a commitment to religious diversity or religious equality, albeit wrapped up in some of the confusion around the debate on multiculturalism

All these conditions and many more create a great opportunity for the Church to focus on its central mission and ministry by finding relevant and appropriate ways to welcome and relate to people who don't know about or have experience of Christianity. But like the shape of the landscape, the discourse is changing fast, and the Church must urgently address not only how to engage with it but also how to act appropriately, beyond the dialogue.

But what do church mission and ministry look like in 21st Century multi-faith Britain?

That's what this book is all about. My prayer is that it will inspire and help you to embrace and include people of different faith identities, while strengthening confidence in your own Christian identity.

Joy Madeiros is Director of Public Policy for Faithworks, the Christian agency dedicated to helping the church engage in holistic mission.

Chapter 1

Introduction: back to the future

'It's easy to see without looking too far that not much in life is
really sacred.'   Bob Dylan

'We used to have 120 children in the Sunday School. We had to hire
another building because the church hall wasn't big enough. Everyone
used to sit very quietly as well, Richard! I can remember to this day the
first non-white person I got to know. She came to our school when I was
about 9 or 10 and she'd come with her family all the way from Kenya'.

This is Anne speaking. She still lives in this area, worships at the
same church, helps with the same Sunday School. The Sunday
School now caters for about 30 children. Anne's sentiments about
church life as the hub of the community in Britain 50 years ago
could be replicated right across the nation.

Times have changed. That same area is now approximately 70%
Muslim, most originating from the Mirpur region of Pakistan.
Anne's friend from Kenya would no longer be the isolated novelty
she then was. Alongside the predominant Muslim community are
Somali Muslims, Hindus, Sikhs, Chinese and asylum seekers from
the Middle East and Africa. This is now my neighbourhood,
too, and I, with Anne, enjoy the local Asian greengrocers, kebab
houses, Bhangra music and sweet stores. Things ain't what they
used to be, and change seems to be the only constant. As I write
this, the local Asian newsagents have just put up a sign in Polish,
advertising foodstuffs catering to the freshest wave of language
and culture mixing in our neighbourhood.

What do all these changes mean for the life and mission of the
British church? We seem reasonably comfortable thinking of the
current national dish as Chicken Tikka Masala. But have we done

anything to alter the ingredients of our witness as Christian communities? Even posing this question might provoke the odd shudder of nervousness. We live at a juncture in history fraught with tension. We are, admittedly, a bit mindful of the cultural imperialism of much of the Victorian-era missionary endeavour. There is a residual guilt-trip that baulks us as Christians looking across at neighbours of other faiths. The events of 9/11 and 7/7 have brought to the fore our deepest fears, and we could be excused for being paralysed by inaction.

Here's a recent snapshot of the faith make-up of Britain, taken from a BBC ICM Survey conducted in 2005:

Christian	= 67%
Muslim	= 3%
Jewish	= 1%
Hindu	= 1%
Sikh	= <1%
Other	= 4%
No Faith	= 22%
Refused	= 1%
Don't know	= <1%

Admittedly, such surveys never present the full picture, and one person's faith might be just another's shorthand for the 'Religion' section in a hospital form. In the 2001 British Census, 'Jedi Knight' was given its own category in the list of religions, as so many people had written this entry in their census returns. Well, may the force be with them! But the BBC ICM Survey also asked about attendance at worship services. The picture this paints seems to be a little closer to the reality of the scene. Of the 67% of the population who would call themselves 'Christian', only 17% attend a service of worship at least once a week. That suggests that about 11% of the British population are attending some kind of Christian worship each week. Looking at the worship patterns of those who called themselves Muslims, over 58% are attending a service at a mosque each week. Over 47% of Sikhs are attending a service of worship at a gurdwara or temple each week. Many of our other faith neighbours declare their faith and support it with a very tangible commitment in communal acts of worship.

However we cut the cake, the visibility of the Christian faith is far from what it used to be in Britain 50 or even 20 years ago. Alongside the obvious cultural and racial differences of the nation is a whole plethora of faiths which bring with them values, perspectives, histories and texts which have to be reckoned with in what we call Britain today.

How on earth do Christian communities appropriately reach out to those of other faiths in such a time as this? This book presumes the very fact that we ought to be reaching out. The challenge is to walk on a journey of interaction with others which somehow enables us to be true to our faith yet appropriately shaped by our experiences and the people we meet. The Christian faith is such that it needs to be embodied in a time and a place: as one theologian put it, for each generation, the good news needs to be *'forwarded to a new address'*. The landscape of Britain in the 21st century therefore requires us to be aware of the mixed baggage of mission history, world politics and multiculturalism in all its guises, as we look in particular to our relationship with those of other faiths.

The New Testament was forged in the furnace of cultural change and interfaith mixing. Many scholars would argue that most of the Old Testament was similarly written, at a time when Jews were rubbing shoulders with others as a minority faith in exile. There are lessons to be learnt from our Scriptures and indeed, I would argue, there is something of *the essence* in our story which involves an interaction with other faiths. The sweep of the biblical narrative is not a smooth one. We might evoke Abraham, called out of Ur to a new land, Jeremiah at the foot of a cesspit in Jerusalem encircled by the armies of Babylon, or Paul under house arrest, writing and teaching a subversive message about a different kind of king and a different kind of kingdom in the very heart of the Roman Empire. All these characters, and more, grappled to hear and enact God's Word in the midst of diversity. Each time, God's Word was not predictable; there were patterns, certainly, but the very vocation of these people of faith often pushed them to places of discomfort. Furthermore, it often led to their rejection by those that should have known better.

We see this supremely in the life of Jesus: the ultimate cross-cultural missionary, God taking on the body and soul of a Jew, caught in the massive affront of a pagan occupation. What did it mean to be a faithful Jew at such a time as this? The answers were unpredictable, brought their own rejection and marginalising, and led to death on the cross. But as with all these men and women of faith, in the place of their vulnerability, at the point of God's goodness taking shape in a time and place, new life came.

It is with this hope that I seek to address our relationship to those of other faiths today: a hope that new life can come. In theological parlance, we would call it 'resurrection'. The theological parlance is more than mere talk of life beyond the grave for the faithful; it speaks of God's possibilities here and now where we often just see darkness and despair. The interface between Christians and other faiths is an arena which, for many, is indeed worthy of despair. For the non-religious observing from the stands, there is a quite understandable feeling of 'a plague on both your houses' after perceived atrocities in the name of religion. Not long after the July 7th bombings in London, I came across this piece:

In the light of recent events, it's really quite frightening to realise the mindset of some of the people who think they have a right to live in a country like Britain.

People who follow a religion that has repeatedly been taken as the basis for hatred and violence towards any that oppose their worldview. People who count as holy, a book that seems to applaud mass murder. The destruction not merely of their military opponents, but innocent civilian women and children.

People who persist in following their religion despite its shameful history. A history that includes innumerable acts of terrorism and racial hatred. A history of oppressing women, keeping them subservient and dictating how they may dress. A religion that has a track record of nations that have been brutally governed by rulers who took it upon themselves to be the voice of their God and to impose ridiculously detailed legislation as to what was permissible in everyday life. A religion that seems to have so often fostered paranoia.

Should we really put up any longer with allowing these people to live amongst us? To share the benefits of our liberal society even though their ultimate allegiance is not to our government but to their invisible worldwide nation?

This surely is a recipe for disaster. The government must act quickly and decisively to deport all Christians.[1]

---

[1] Quoted by kind permission of the author, Rev Richard White

We think we have the author taped and his prejudices under-lined, but the force of the punch-line reveals our own prejudice. As Christians, we so often fail to see our errors and the monstrous acts of violence committed in the name of and in pursuit of the Christian faith. While working in North Africa, I was frequently shocked at how often the Crusades came into the conversation. The legacy of church-sponsored invasion to recapture holy sites nearly seven hundred years before was a continuing reality. And when the President of the United States invokes the word 'crusade' in a war against terrorism, the shudders amongst Muslim nations and in Muslim communities in Britain are palpable. Even a cursory glance at our own history must give us pause for thought before making sweeping judgements about another faith.

Let us return to the micro-level of local church; to districts such as Anne's with a majority Muslim community. To workplaces in our cities where we rub shoulders with those of other faiths and to our universities, packed with diversity. The background noise is alarming yet we are called to be witnesses to the world, to offer hope and a distinctiveness centred on Christ. What should con-temporary church life in its engagement with those of other faiths look like while the background noise of the so-called 'clash of civil-isations' assaults all our senses?

I write this with a great deal of presumption: to offer a way forward that seeks to be true to the uniqueness of the Christian faith and holding to the particularity of Christ. Yet this truthfulness to Christ requires our ability to be necessarily shaped by our own context and humbly to see the good in 'the other'. There seems to be a simplistic drift in much of the Christian literature and pro-nouncements on Christian-other faith relations towards either a benign but bland smoothing over of all our differences or a zealous but arrogant activism. I trust that what I share will be helpful in out-lining a thoroughly Christian position which leaves us all in some discomfort while exhilarated by new hope and fresh possibilities.

Other publications should be sought for an overview of the beliefs of other faiths. And I hope that after reading this, you will run to your bookshops and libraries trawling for information on the religions you encounter. It is not the role of this book to intro-duce the elements of world religions to Christians. Each chapter, as appropriate, will signpost sources for further reading on specific faiths. But my conviction is that we need a better understanding of our own faith before we jump towards a necessary understanding of other religions. I envisage this effort to be a resource for Christians living and working alongside other faiths so that they themselves become confident in building upon biblical foundations to be neighbours, witnesses, friends and partners. I will endeavour to make sense of some of the background noise and to give pointers and suggestions to the kinds of ministry Christian communities could be having at this time.

This journey requires us to look at the whole nature of 'religions', to take a fresh view of what we mean by the 'gospel': literally, our 'good news'. In a book encouraging application, then, there are key arenas such as evangelism, community service, youth work and politics which demand attention. Each chapter will offer space for biblical reflection, worship, prayer and action. This structure is not offered merely to enable the book to be studied in a group format or to provide some novelty. It is to underline, whether individually or in a group, that the application of our faith to the real-world issues of witness in a multi-faith context demands the rigour of Christian worship. As we pray in our world, as we reflect on our key text, commit ourselves to our Creator and go forth in Spirit-empowered deeds, then we keep to our calling, however vulnerable and risky the path may seem.

Following the theme of 'Distinctly Welcoming', there will be space to reflect on a Bible passage ('A La Carte' 🍽️), to respond in prayer and worship ('Soundtrack' 🎧) and to commit to action ('Takeaway' 🛵). This system attempts to model the core commitment of this book: that our engagement with culture demands of us a corresponding engagement with the Bible and a responsiveness in worship and prayer. As our Christian story becomes rooted in a context and a lived reality, we then allow ourselves to be shaped into authentic practitioners of God's life in the world. There will also be suggestions for follow-up resources: detailed books ('Banquet' 🏠), easier introductions ('Healthy Appetisers' 🍎) and web resouces ('Virtual Food' 🖱️).

Some time ago, I facilitated a meeting between a group of trainee missionaries and a gathering of mosque imams. The imams were well known to local Christian leaders and there had been a history of exchanges and dialogues between the two groups for some years. However, this was the first time that we had introduced Christian missionaries to them. These missionaries, coincidentally, were all going to work in Muslim countries. I asked them to share the reasons for such career decisions. All of them were professionals, giving up comfortable positions in Britain, and all shared stories of genuine Christian conviction and service to the poor and marginalised of other nations. It was a momentous meeting because the Muslim leaders were hearing stories of deep faith from younger British Christians. Such stories are often quite alien to our Muslim neighbours, more familiar with the licence and immorality of the nominally Christian West.

I then threw the conversation over to the imams: 'So, then, what would you like to say to these Christian missionaries as they settle in Muslim countries?' The eldest imam, straining at the leash, pointed a bony finger at each of them and said, 'I would like to ask why you are going abroad, because this country is godless and needs people like you.' We had risked an open conversation where we would be being utterly true to ourselves as Christians, in the context of trusting relationship. Muslim leaders had heard surprising and rare stories of godly faithfulness from young Christians. We, in turn, had heard a challenge and a reminder about the godlessness at the heart of our own society. This small exchange exemplifies something to which we should be aspiring: mutual story-telling, a willingness to be challenged and a truthfulness about who we are.

There is risk in this because genuine relationships are not predictable. But it is genuine relationships which are currently desperately needed between Christians and those of other faiths. Relationships cannot be programmed and replicated, still less packaged in a paint-by-numbers guide. Relationships of any maturity look unblinkingly at the conflicts, take account of histories but choose to work through them. It is for this reason that I tentatively regard this book as a resource: a resource to give shape to productive encounters.

Coming full circle, I write in the confidence that our core text, the Bible, gives us more than clues, should we choose to grapple with it in all its provocativeness. When Bob Dylan was penning the lyrics quoted at the start of this introduction, he was bemoaning the commodity which faith had become. We would do well to beware the labels of religion and to begin this journey seeking as our benchmark a likeness to Christ. As we recognise Jesus as the very imprint of God, we are able to see Jesus not as the founder of one of any number of religions, but the enabler and summation of God's life on earth. God refuses to be boxed in, confined and defined by us. As soon as we box God in, we end up worshipping an idol of our own making. The repercussions of Jesus' own life are testimony to our tendency to domesticate our Saviour. He was domesticated and confined to the severe limits of a cross, but wonderfully, he broke free from those confines and continues to do so today.

As we look across our various divides to our neighbours in multi-faith Britain, we must come in diffidence, that the profane be made sacred again. This journey is not just one on which a world in captivity to religious division needs to embark; it is a journey vital to the very integrity of our Christian faith.

A LA CARTE 🍽 – Matthew 5–7

Take time to read the whole of what is known as the Sermon on the Mount. You may want to read this sermon of Jesus a number of times over a few weeks. Enter into the story itself; read it as an imaginative contemplation. Picture yourself there, as one of the characters. You might be a disciple of Jesus, an ordinary Jew hearing this new preacher, a Roman soldier standing by watching for any trouble and listening out for subversive messages. You could be a religious leader, nervous about the direction of the ministry of this teacher from Nazareth and concerned to keep Jews along strict lines of observance which keep the history and faith of the nation alive. You may be a Zealot, a rebel waiting for the right time to use a leader who would galvanise the people in rebellion against the Romans. The 'background noise' of Jesus' sermon is the troubled nation of Israel, its history of blessing from Yahweh with all its promise, and now its humiliated status under the Roman Empire. 'Where is our God now?' would be a familiar cry of the faithful Jew. The choices seem stark: rebellion, compromise or exclusivism. Take time to sum up the likely smells and sights of the scene, identify your own concerns as one of the bystanders and reflect on your feelings as you hear this radical teacher. Note that the 'persecuted', those asked for their cloaks, those struck on the right cheek or instructed to carry a load for a mile, would be very familiar scenarios for Jews under Roman occupation. And note the subtle subversion of Jesus' advice to offer up the left cheek, thus standing as an equal to the Roman. Or to go the extra mile in contravention of a Roman soldier's regulations, and letting the suitor have the cloak (or, literally, undergarment) to the shame of those responsible.

1. *What were your feelings as you read this sermon through the eyes of one of the bystanders?*

2. *What surprised you about your reactions?*
3. *What did this reveal to you about the character and ministry of Jesus?*
4. *How might this sermon and your reactions to it be helpful in looking at Christians' relations with those of other faiths?*

SOUNDTRACK 🎧

Write a poem or draw a picture relating to the scene from the Sermon on the Mount on which you meditated. The picture can be expressive: just colours and shapes. If you find poetry or art too difficult, write a 'letter to God'. Express the feelings you experienced from this scene in some way. Give them to God with thanks, both the insights and comfort, and the shocks and discomfort. Commit to allowing Jesus, in all his dangerousness, to be Lord.

Gracious Father, we come to you seeking to be part of your story. We know that your story is replete with love, abounds in peace and glitters with joy. But we also know that entering into your story means entering into your pain. We are sorry for boxing you in so that, in our efforts to follow you, we have written our own conclusions. Be among us, Lord, prise our hands open that we may allow you to write our endings and in those endings discover new beginnings. To the glory of Jesus, who broke the Sabbath traditions, touched the unclean and delighted in the faith of the foreigner. Amen.

TAKEAWAY 🏍

Research another faith, ideally the one you are most likely to encounter, perhaps through a neighbour or work colleague, but make sure you incorporate relationships in this quest. Seek authoritative sources from that other faith to find out about the beliefs of this religion. Check websites, ask friends or neighbours and visit bookshops. If you live in a city with a large Muslim population, for example, visit a Muslim bookshop and ask about Muslims' beliefs and see what subjects are interesting them. Decide to be open and curious about the beliefs of others, and begin a process of assessing areas of commonality and difference.

BANQUET ⛺

V Ramachandra *Faiths in Conflict? Christian Integrity in a Multicultural World* (IVP, 1999)

HEALTHY APPETISERS

Ida Glaser and Shaylesh Raja *Sharing the Salt*, a gentle intro-duction and encouragement to engagement with people of different faiths, published by Scripture Union, ISBN 1 85999 307 9, copies still available from Kitab Oriental Books, Satis@kitab.org.uk

Cross and Crescent (on Islam) available from Faith to Faith, www.faithtofaith.org.uk

Cross and Khalsa (on Sikhism) available from Faith to Faith, www.faithtofaith.org.uk

Cross and Lotus (on Buddhism) available from Faith to Faith, www.faithtofaith.org.uk

Cross and New Age Spirituality (on New Age thinking) available from Faith to Faith, www.faithtofaith.org.uk

Christ and the Tao (on Chinese religions) available from Faith to Faith, www.faithtofaith.org.uk

Friendship First – the Manual (on Islam) available from www.advancebookshop.co.uk

VIRTUAL FOOD

Faith to Faith, www.faithtofaith.org.uk

Church Mission Society, www.cms-uk.org

BBC Religions – http://www.bbc.co.uk/religion/religions/ for easy access to a whole range of information on different religions includ-ing stories of faith from respective adherents.

Chapter 2

Give me Back my Mission

'Once in a while you get shown the light in the strangest of places if you look at it right'.   Jerry Garcia

John Wimber, the founder of the Vineyard church movement, heralded a visit to Britain in the early 1980s with a prophecy to the British simply stating, 'Give me back my church'. It resonated with scores of Christians who recognised the gulf between a Bible bristling with God's transcendence and the experience of a church that seemed devoid of any sense of encounter with the Holy Spirit. I'd like to take the phrase a stage further and suggest that we need to see something of the *full* scope of the Holy Spirit and place the mission of the church within God's wider work: give me back my mission!

Theologians have the neat Latin phrase, the *missio dei*, the mission of God, for underlining that the church is only a part of what God does in the world. It's an important motif for reminding ourselves as Christians that we are servants of God in his mission, and not masters of this mission. This concept finds itself evidenced throughout scripture and is a jolt to the Messiah-complexes which litter churches and missionary endeavours.

Hebrews 11 takes us on a whistle-stop tour of men and women who continue the great story of faith in Yahweh. Rahab gleams as the example of the non-Jew who served God's purposes, exhibiting a faith proven by her actions to protect the spies. Other cameos glisten in the Old Testament such as Naaman, the commander of the armies of the pagan king of Aram. It is stressed that God had used Naaman to bring victory to Aram, and his story evokes something of the man's integrity and openhearted faith from within a foreign religion. Elisha freely blesses Naaman with healing ascribed to Yahweh. Any decision to worship the god of Israel comes later. King Cyrus, the Persian empire-builder and leader of a pagan nation repeatedly the bane of Israel, is chosen as God's vehicle for his purposes in the region. I could go on: the point is that God chooses to work with, bless and involve those outside the 'normal' boundaries of his people to fulfil his purposes.

Jesus' own ministry was characterised by a controversial trait of highlighting the faith and obedience of those outside the Jewish religion. It didn't make him too popular! Jesus was also often despairing of the faith of those supposedly at the heart of God's purposes. Here are just three examples from actual encounters, without even looking at the thinly disguised challenges in so many of the parables:

1. Matthew 8:5–13 and Luke 7:1–10 – a Roman centurion is commended for his faith and healed. Jesus says, 'I have not found anyone in Israel with such great faith. I say to you that many will come from the east and the west, and will take their places at the feast with Abraham, Isaac and Jacob in the kingdom of heaven.' It seems that the centurion had gained the respect of local Jews and shown his love for the people by even building the local synagogue.
2. Luke 10:1–24 – Jesus commissions 72 to visit towns throughout Israel, teaching and healing the sick. Anticipating rejection from some places, he advises, 'Woe to you, Korazin! Woe to you, Bethsaida! For if the miracles that were performed in you had been performed in Tyre and Sidon, they would have repented long ago… But it will be more bearable for Tyre and Sidon at the judgement than for you.'
3. Luke 17:11–19 – Jesus heals ten leprosy sufferers and only one, a Samaritan, returns to give him thanks. Jesus asks, 'Were not all ten cleansed? Where are the other nine? Was no-one found to return and give praise to God except this foreigner?' Jesus then says, 'Rise and go; your faith has made you well,' as if there were a further healing, a blessing, a forgiveness for the Samaritan who had given thanks.

Perhaps the finest New Testament example of what I shall call 'faith beyond the boundaries' is that of Cornelius in Acts 10. Here is a Roman centurion who is termed 'God-fearing'. He prays regularly and demonstrates this faith in God by giving generously to the poor. In these two ways, Cornelius somehow pleases God, though a rank outsider in terms of his status as a non-Jew and in complete ignorance of who Jesus was. For Peter to visit Cornelius in his home went against the very fibre of his upbringing, his faith and all that he had been taught as a Jew. Peter needed three visions to take on board the message that he was to visit this Roman centurion.

It's worth asking at what point God was listening to Cornelius' prayers and at work in Cornelius' life. We may even speculate as to what would have happened if Cornelius had died while Peter was *en route* to his house; would Cornelius have been assured of new life in Christ? The truth is that these questions are not ours to ask and actually distract us from the heart of the story. However, these are the kinds of question in which we, as Christians, do get bogged down. Too often, in our distraction, we miss out on what God is actually doing. The concept of God's mission, not ours, means that the story of Cornelius should be no surprise to us. It may be uncomfortable: it may make the journey of Christian witness less predictable and suggest that we may have to overcome some of our own resistance to God on the way. But God is God and will move, by his Spirit, speaking to people, engineering encounters, listening to the cries and prayers of all sorts of odd outsiders in ways that God is completely at liberty to do.

This foundation of mission is, I believe, crucial to our understanding of those of other faiths. Once we see God, untamed, unconfined, working in and beyond the church, the way we approach and pray for others will inevitably shift.

Naturally enough, we would then ask ourselves, 'So what about salvation?' However much we might like to sidle around the issue, we have to address this nagging question. It can't help but inform our relationships with Muslims, Hindus, Sikhs or anyone else outside the church. I'd like to present an overview of the traditional responses to this question, then suggest a fresher way forward which allows us to hold on to Jesus' uniqueness yet incorporates the sense of God at work beyond the boundaries.

'There is a kingdom, there is a king and he lives without and he lives within'. Nick Cave

1. *Exclusivism* – this is the term given to the traditional conservative evangelical position. Quoting Jesus' words, 'I am the way the truth and the life, no one comes to the Father but by me' (John 14:6), it reflects the view that a relationship with God and new life beyond death is only possible after a personal commitment to Christ. The following diagram attempts to illustrate the boundaries of the exclusivist view. There is a clear line between those who are 'in' and those who are 'out'. The church contains those who are saved and to step into the circle of those who have discovered the truth requires that explicit beliefs in Jesus are expressed. There may be knotty discussions about whether baptism, membership, a specific conversion experience or a sequence of significant events constitute the correct rite of passage. Notwithstanding those things, a picture of Christianity in its relation to other faiths and no faith are essentially stark and clear-cut in this model:

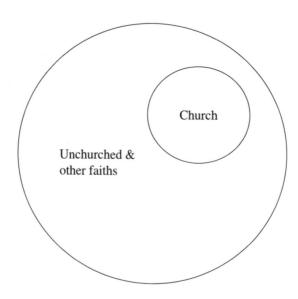

2. *Inclusivism* – this flows from the exclusivist position but allows for the inclusion of '*some others*' into God's salvation plan. It reflects the idea of 'God-fearers' in scripture and recognises individuals outside the traditional confines of faith whom God has embraced, perhaps through their actions or heartfelt prayers.

Romans 1:20 may be a key verse here, describing God's revelation in creation, suggesting that people are able, at least to some extent, to discern God's will through the created order. So as well as faith in Christ, there may be others who have had no opportunity to hear the good news but whom God affirms because of their response to the revelation they did receive.

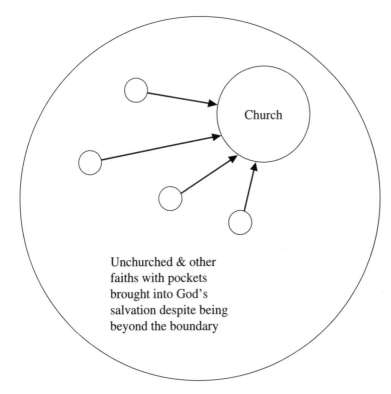

Church

Unchurched & other faiths with pockets brought into God's salvation despite being beyond the boundary

3. *Pluralism* – this is the classical liberal view of salvation. All faiths are but specific revelations of a greater good or sense of the divine. We can only know in part and our portion of knowledge is no more valid and real than anyone else's. In the imagery of John Hick, our grasp of the divine is like feeling an elephant in a dark room. What we grasp hold of speaks of something but it is incomplete and insufficient and requires us not to elevate our knowledge above another's. Another illustration of this might be different paths up a mountainside. They are different routes but the same God, like

the mountain, is the destination of all these alternatives. The words of Psalm 24:1 are taken by some as reflecting the emphasis of the pluralist tradition: 'The earth is the Lord's, and everything in it, the world and all who live in it.'

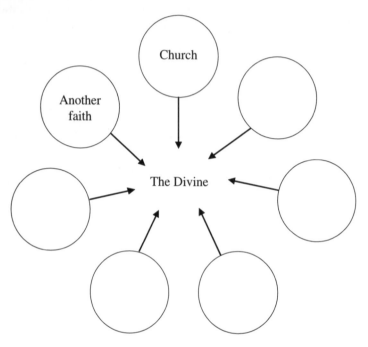

All three perspectives contain elements of truth which we see in Scripture; they each reflect something of what we know of God. Many of us hold on to the truth that it is in Jesus that God and salvation are fully revealed and sympathise with something of the *exclusivist* approach. To know Christ is to know God. His life, death and resurrection are vital to the newness for which the world is desperate. However, there is clearly a tradition and precedent for God's embracing and affirming the prayers and actions of those outside the household of faith, and we may want to recognise something of the *inclusivist* view. I have to be honest here and say that I do struggle with the *pluralist* tradition. I can't put the beliefs and prophets of other faiths on an equal footing with the Bible and with the core of my faith, Jesus. But even in this model, we recognise that God's desire is to love and bless all people, that mercy triumphs over judgement and that what we know is incomplete.

Each of these pictures, and I admit they are simplistic pictures, answers different questions. If you want an answer to the question, 'Is Jesus the source of life, central to the whole of creation?' or 'Is Jesus' death and resurrection the only hope for the world?', then I give my answer as an exclusivist. If you want to answer the question, 'Will we find only Christians in heaven?', I answer as an inclusivist. If you ask the question, 'Is God moving across the whole world and active in all cultures, peoples and places?', then I give a pluralist answer.

Hold on there a minute! Are you telling me to change years of thinking about other faiths and who goes to heaven and who goes to hell?

No, I'm just asking you to come at the issue from a different place. I don't mind if you still call yourself an exclusivist or an inclusivist (I struggle with the pluralist option that all roads lead to God though!). What I'm looking to do is to get people to step back and not view other faiths primarily in terms of something that is only God's decision. The question of salvation is still vitally important, but let's look at what the Bible says should influence our attitudes and behaviour first and foremost ... Go with me on this one!

At the end of the day, I find all these approaches deeply unsatisfactory as a defining frame for how we relate to other faiths. If pressed, I would go for the *inclusivist* option, but it is so unclear what beliefs or actions allow people 'in'. The pluralist has good grounds for dragging you towards a slippery relativism that ceases to be what I recognise as the Christian faith. It also seems quite patronising to stand within your own circle, picking out the best in others' religions as if graciously bestowing marks on pupils who 'could do better'.

I think we're on far safer ground by owning that this scheme of thought is not necessarily a biblical given for how we understand the Christian faith in relation to other faiths. It owes much more to a modernist world view that seeks to make human beings the ultimate and not God. Let's have a bit of social history.

Since the European Enlightenment and the grand project of industrialisation, our corporate story has included a sense of how we can be architects of a better future, a future that can be reasoned out and objectified. Appropriately, because the good news of Christ needs to be fleshed out in the clothes and language of each place and generation, the Church has provided its own version of this story. So we can be architects of a better future by believing a certain set of rational arguments about sin, God, Jesus and his work on the cross. Assent to this system of beliefs allows access to that better future, a future that you cannot see at present, but a future nonetheless.

This works well when the 'competition' is just humanism: the belief that what we see, touch, know and can verify by science is all that there is. 'Good' choices flow from what is rationally regarded as good and the more we know, the more likely we are to make the world a better place. Two world wars, a very scientific genocide of the Jews and the spectre of ecological disaster have all helped to leave this vision in tatters. Advances in science, too, have presented us with a world which cannot be reduced to simple cause and effect. Knowledge, reality and history are hugely fluid concepts and less 'empirical' than was previously thought.

Christianity finds itself in a very different landscape. Notions of authority, community and the way we approach our texts are all being challenged. There is a new openness to the spiritual and mystical, and a willingness to embrace the miraculous in Scripture with which scientific humanists would struggle. But this openness includes an openness to 'whatever works' in any number of faith practices: superstitions, hunches and experiments which now intermingle in our societies. The 'whatever generation' is OK with faith but is it the faith of the Christian tradition? In the words of one of the prophets of post-modernism, Jean-Francois Lyotard, there is an 'incredulity to the meta-narrative'. That's posh philosopher-speak for: 'There's no big story; just make it up as you go along'.

As the haloes of scientists, politicians, doctors, teachers and business leaders have been removed, whether by food scares, continued wars, irreparable damage to the environment or exposés of private lives, church leaders, too, have come under the microscope. In Britain, I can guarantee that a word association game of 'vicar' played with someone who never came to church would produce the response, 'child abuse'. If not, they might imagine a

Dick Emery style middle-aged irrelevance spluttering over his afternoon tea. We might be forgiven for believing that all our sacred cows are now dead. It seems that death itself remains the last taboo. The church has a responsibility to name and act out our hope of new life, a new life that begins this side of death and overcomes it.

Knowledge itself as a concept has undergone its own revolution and seems to be understood in more relational terms. It is not merely an item to be ticked off in a checklist in the brain but is something held in community, dependent upon trust. It requires credibility from actions worked out by groups and in this way, carries its power.

All these developments are unsettling and we can see the troubled negotiation of these even *within* our churches. Have you noticed that these days we're all a bit suspicious of big powerful church leaders arriving with a fanfare and promising all the answers? And churches are recognising that communication has to include stories, visuals, and clips from films. The message we carry is far deeper and more tangible than a simple set of ideas. It's a tougher call to make the message count in the world we live in. However, I'm excited because – and this may sound weird – this is much closer to the context from which the New Testament was written. We are living in an age when Christianity is just one of many 'bids' out there. True knowledge is not bestowed just because it appears in a textbook; real authority is not demonstrated by pulling rank. The New Testament was written in a period of profound change from within the Roman Empire, an empire with its 'big story' of allegiance to the Emperor but its multiple stories of gods and goddesses, of conquered lands with their own beliefs and practices, with the realities of life as citizen, slave and foreigner. The supernatural and the mystical vied with philosophy, reason and science and the *Pax Romana* and its consequent impact on trade provided an ever-rich recycling of languages, ideas and faiths.

At the heart of the empire, as we glimpse Paul writing his final letters from imprisonment in Rome, is a community which might be regarded as a very odd assortment: Jew and Gentile, professional, educated, rich and poor, together fashioning the foundations of the church. They have no position to command the ear of the Empire; in fact, allegiance to the faith often leads to death. But something of the life and witness of these Christians exhibits a different kind of authority. Their stories coalesce into the big story of God's dealings with the world and rock the Empire to its core.

There are very many parallels from which we can draw in this time of cultural change, and it gives us scope more effectively to mine the Bible for resources in our churches. The good news of Christ, as in every age, both speaks into the culture and defies it. So, as the early church emphasised the Lordship of Jesus, at a time when the Roman Emperor was 'Lord', there was a simultaneous use of language and imagery familiar to that time, with an undermining of how that was commonly understood. For someone in the first century, to choose 'Jesus is Lord' as an alternative to the more common allegiance 'Caesar is Lord' had massive implications. It meant more than opting for a different mental belief system. If Caesar was Lord, he owned your destiny. Your rights as a Roman citizen meant that wherever you were in the Empire, whether in Rome, Corinth, Palestine or Ephesus, you were guaranteed certain privileges and freedoms. Your family, servants, slaves, the whole of your household, were also subject to the same allegiance to which you were sworn. Saying that 'Caesar is Lord' is not about you and what you get. In fact, you could not *'get'* citizenship; it could only be given to you. Slaves in the Roman Empire were owned, and their allegiance was a *fait accompli*. If Caesar wished to pronounce on your execution, as a Roman citizen, then he could; it was his right. Being a Roman showed to whom you belonged, of which community you were a part, to what history you were joined and to what future you were committed.

A conquered city would often contain a statue of the Emperor as an affirmation that the city belonged to another kingdom. It bore the imprint and image of the owner. When we read in the Bible of humanity 'bearing the imprint of God', there is more than a family likeness to be read into this concept. We belong to God and the early church, and Christians everywhere are living lives which reveal our true ownership and our real kingdom.

So to define the Christian faith in the limited terms of the salvation of human souls seems to water down the whole concept of Lordship. We are not the ultimate point of faith; our destinies do not dictate to God. Rather, we are signs and forerunners ('image-bearers') of the kingdom that has come, is coming and is centred on Christ. It is 'all about Jesus' and encompasses people, places, institutions, families, the earth and the animal kingdom. This is truly good news and it is cosmic! The scale is grand and it vies with, contradicts and ultimately supersedes all other empires. Kings, princes, multi-nationals, governments, patriarchs are all would-be powers in the light of God's reign over everything.

Let's look at all the diagrams again: what we are doing when we define our faith in the light of other faiths in these ways is making humanity the central point of Christianity. The distinguishing marks of a faith become what 'we believe', what creeds *we* write, what membership *we* set. In the words of the Bishop of Durham, Tom Wright, Christianity is 'not a new way of being religious'. God, as revealed in Christ, should be our start and finish point. Once we go down the route of defining our faith by *our* destiny, we are actually playing the game of the modernists who put human beings at the centre of the cosmos.

What we need to consider is a perspective on our relationship to other faiths which is framed by God's mission for the world and the heart of God's purposes for the world. Stepping back and reflecting on how we define our faith and what we believe about our religions is not merely an academic exercise. True, there are rainforests of books devoted to this topic at an academic level, but I write this as a practitioner, someone passionate about seeing churches live out the Christian story in our neighbourhoods. As we are able to take God's perspective on our relationship with the world and other faiths, I believe we are in a better position to be faithful to God in the mission that he leads.

DISTINCTLY WELCOMING TIPS:

- be less concerned about who is 'in' and who is 'out' and more concerned about the question, 'how does God want me to act towards this person or in this situation?'
- be true to your beliefs, honest about your convictions, public about what Jesus means to you.
- look at people and the world with expectancy and hope.
- when you see signs of the kingdom of God, wherever and in whomever, give thanks to God because every good and perfect gift comes from him.
- be wary of taming God, pinning him down, making salvation something smaller than it actually is.

– remember to keep shifting the outlook away from the priority of mere numbers to the bigger question of 'What is God doing?'

A LA CARTE 🍽 – Acts 10

Read the story of Peter's encounter with the centurion Cornelius. While I was in North Africa, I had the immense privilege of meeting local Muslims who had come to a belief in Christ through having dreams. One man told me of dreaming of walking along a road. Coming to a crossroads, he was confused about which way to turn when a man spoke to him at the crossroads, 'Ask the Englishman at work to show you the way'. I'd heard of tales like this, marvelled at the dreams and visions but never come face to face with the reality. What struck me forcefully, and what continues to shape my ministry back in Britain, is that the vision was not to 'help out' missionaries such as me. From a distance, excited by tales of the Holy Spirit working, it seemed that these dreams and visions were sent to bring success to local missionaries. The reality is far more profound and significant, I believe. God is constantly answering the prayers and petitions of so many people of other faiths. The challenge is whether Christians are available, present, listening and relating in such a way that these prayers can be brought to full fruition in encountering Christ. Cornelius' vision of the angel is an example of God responding to a faithful man's prayer in just this way. Of course, Acts 10 has a unique and particularly significant purpose in shifting Peter's perception of the scope of the gospel message but the acceptance of Cornelius' worship by God precedes all that.

1. *Think of your work colleagues, neighbours, some of your family. Do we imagine them ever 'crying to God', praying in some way. Do you think God ever answers their prayers? And the prayers of those of other faiths you know – what do you think is happening when they pray?*
2. *Peter learned a profound lesson from Cornelius that day. What have you learnt from those of other faiths? Have you ever grown close to God by encountering someone of another faith? Is that/should that be possible?*
3. *Cornelius needed only the one vision while Peter needed three visions to be persuaded that God was saying something. To what extent are you aware that Christians can be more resistant to what God is saying than are others outside the church?*

4. *Going back to the three models of Christianity and religions. Where would you try to fit Cornelius in this schema? Do you agree that another way of looking at religions is needed?*

SOUNDTRACK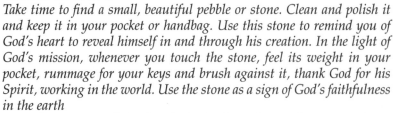

Take time to find a small, beautiful pebble or stone. Clean and polish it and keep it in your pocket or handbag. Use this stone to remind you of God's heart to reveal himself in and through his creation. In the light of God's mission, whenever you touch the stone, feel its weight in your pocket, rummage for your keys and brush against it, thank God for his Spirit, working in the world. Use the stone as a sign of God's faithfulness in the earth

Lord Jesus, you delighted in the faith of outsiders. Help me to rejoice in signs of your goodness in places I might least expect. I thank you Lord, so much, that your purposes do not depend on me and what I do for you. But thank you that you choose to involve me. Give me hands and a heart open to the work of your Holy Spirit. Amen.

TAKEAWAY

Offer to pray for friends or neighbours, whether they have a faith or not. If they do have a faith, ask them what they pray for and ask if you can pray for them, too. Treat their prayer life and requests seriously and with respect and prepare to journey with them as you pray for them and share how God may be speaking to them.

BANQUET

Michael Barnes *Theology and the Dialogue of Religions* (Cambridge University Press, 2002)

HEALTHY APPETISERS

Ida Glaser *The Bible and Other Faiths – what does the Lord require of us?* (IVP, 2005)

VIRTUAL FOOD

Faith to Faith www.faithtofaith.org.uk for downloadable reading lists and articles

Chapter 3

No Limits; Just Edges: Distinctive Faith

'So, so you think you can tell
Heaven from hell,
Blue skies from pain?
Can you tell a green field
From a cold steel rail?
A smile from a veil?
Do you think you can tell?'   (Pink Floyd)

Apart from a strange and eclectic love of music, I enjoy art and particularly the rollercoaster ride that is modern art, in all its joys and ridiculousness. As a family, we had the privilege of a holiday to Venice some years ago, and visited the fabulous Peggy Guggenheim Museum during an exhibition of Jackson Pollock's work. His paintings have always held a fascination for me. They seem utterly chaotic with their dripped-oil effects and swirls, but they transmit an amazing beauty. The exhibition's title was coined by an early art critic of Jackson Pollock's work: *No Limits, Just Edges.*

This phrase, however nonsensical, best sums up my understanding of God's kingdom and its boundaries. In one sense, there are absolutely no boundaries; there is no way we can parcel out, define and determine them; that is God's prerogative and his only. However, throughout Scripture, there is a clear divide between life and death, between the kingdom of light and the kingdom of darkness. A judgement and a separation clearly exist between the two kingdoms, the latter resulting in destruction.

We hold a tension as we follow the path of God in this world, knowing him with us and committing to his Word and with his people the church, while not always being able to predetermine where we will find God at work or among whom we will experience his life. Our responsibilities lie in working out our worship, through Christ, and loving our neighbours as ourselves. The way we relate, whether we express that love, matters more than our ability to put people in one camp or another. There are no limits to God's goodness, nowhere that we might be surprised to find his kingdom active. But there are edges; there is darkness, suffering, pain and brokenness. I believe our grasp of Christianity in relation to other faiths needs to take on a different shape from the labels of exclusivism, inclusivism and pluralism. For me, this shape can be found in the core distinctiveness of the Christian faith.

In the previous chapter, I tantalisingly suggested that I wanted to share with you a solution to the complex problem of being a Christian in a multi-faith, multicultural world. I indicated that there could be a fresher way forward which allows us to hold onto Jesus' uniqueness yet incorporate the sense of God at work beyond the boundaries.

Here goes. . . but first, by way of background, just a few more paragraphs about difference and about our understanding of faith as a difference.

Have you ever noticed that being 'cool' is as much about being the same as others as it is about being different? Perversely, we seem to want to wear clothes with the same brand name on them while at the same time, we want to be recognised and treated equally for our differences. Whether young or old, male or female, gay or straight, religious or non religious we are, as a society, increasingly learning to recognise and respect difference, despite our love of brand names.

In our workplaces, equal opportunities and diversity policies rightly encourage us to treat colleagues fairly and to embrace difference. Cohesion and integration are some of the buzz words for central and local government. Even ten years ago, there was not the scale of debate we are experiencing today about equality and society's expectations of fairness. That a football manager is now expected to resign following an incident involving sexist or racist comments is a sign of some of the progress we have made.

Or is it? Is this as true for faith as it is for gender and race or any of the other categories of diversity such as age, sexual orientation, ethnicity or disability? OK, there have been many very positive changes in relation to faith in the last few years. Religious belief is now protected as part of discrimination and religious hatred legislation; freedom to express religious belief is one of the pillars of the Charter for Human Rights; and central government has worked hard to ensure that local faith groups are encouraged to be active members of local partnerships.

But on the other hand, we have to admit that faith as a category of difference is still a major problem. The truth is that, as a nation, we still find it difficult to understand what it means to have a faith or to live by faith. Unless we are with friends, we can still be diffident about owning up to what motivates us. Yes, religious education is still on the school curriculum but that's very different from learning about faith and what it means to have a faith motivation. Yes, it's true that nearly 20% of the Voluntary and Community Sector are faith-based, but the sector is still struggling to know how to handle the faith of faith-based organisations. Any political figure who discloses a faith is put on the critical list by the media. Anyone who operates in public from a faith perspective is made out to be an oddity or suspicious. Faith is best relegated to the private matters league. Even though there seems to be a growing interest in spirituality, there is widespread ignorance and suspicion about faith motivation.

So while we cannot deny the fact that faith is an aspect of millions of people's identities in the UK – or, for those who want to get technical, that faith is very definitely a category of the UK's equality and diversity agenda – we all know that there is nevertheless a very limited and shallow understanding of what it means to have a faith.

As a nation, despite our long and substantial history of being a Christian nation, the truth is that we don't really know what to do with faith. A fascination about it which comes out of a genuine ignorance is sometimes mixed up with a misplaced fear resulting in a genuine confusion about the role and validity of faith in public life. Basically, it's a mess.

And right in the middle of that mess is the 64 million dollar question: how, as a Christian, do I relate to the people who live right next door who have a different faith from mine? How is it possible to treat a person of another faith the same as we would treat a Christian when we confidently claim that Christianity has the unique truth? It would surely be being dishonest to respect their religion as being equal to Christianity, wouldn't it?

As a response to this question, I want to introduce you to the idea of *distinctive faith*. In order to do this, I would like you to think about how you feel when a good friend of yours or your married partner does something you don't like or with which you disagree.

Knowing myself, I generally behave in one of two ways. I either try to change the behaviour by challenging it and criticising it or I try to ignore it and hope it goes away. In other words, my focus becomes fixed on the other person – I want him to change and I do this by challenging him or by concentrating on ignoring him.

Why do I react in this way? It's obvious, isn't it? When someone who matters to you does something you don't agree with, it creates a threat to the relationship. And that sets up a fight or flight reaction. The problem is that if these approaches don't sort things out, you have to decide whether you can live with the change in your partner or live without the relationship.

While you might have started out by trying to challenge the situation or behave as if it did not exist, if the other person won't change, you can only resolve it by dealing with yourself in the end, and being clear about what you think is important for you.

What has this to do with how Christians relate to people of different faiths? Everything. The faith landscape in the UK has changed significantly over the last few decades. Faith communities from all over the world have found their home in Britain and, suddenly, we face not just our own questions about the relationship of Christianity to other faiths but questions from society about how the relationship should work. And to make matters worse, we're on the back foot because we've been asleep, dozing away in a darkroom of complacency where there have been very few, if any, challenges to our faith identity.

Now, it's all very different; we have to decide how to respond but are not sure what to make of it all. So we default into normal behaviour. Some of us go into challenge mode, criticising the fact that other faith groups dominate the Christian faith – after all, we were here first and this nation has a long and strong Christian heritage. Others try to carry on as normal, behaving as if nothing has changed. But we know deep down that fight or flight is not the answer. Let's face it, it hasn't changed the situation back to what it was – and I'm not suggesting that would be a good thing, anyway. No, we need to come to terms with the fact that the faith landscape has changed and get to grips with how to handle it.

Back to your relationship. If you want to stay in it, I want to suggest that your relationship works better when both of you know who you are, what matters to you and what you want. You might not be in agreement that you want the same thing and it might be difficult to resolve the differences but at least you both know what makes the other one happy and you will try to accommodate each other.

If, on the other hand, one of you has no idea what you want or assumes that you know the wishes of the other without asking, both of you will soon find the relationship frustrating and unsatisfying. When one partner fails to acknowledge who he/she is, what matters to him/her and take responsibility for it, both partners suffer in the end. Knowing who you are is essential to a healthy relationship.

It's the same with someone of a different faith. Knowing how your faith affects your identity is the starting point for crossing the divide that separates you and building a relationship. You can never know what it means for another person to have a faith identity; you can only ever really know what it means for yourself. Taking responsibility for yourself and understanding your own faith is the key ingredient. If you don't start here, where else?

This is what I would call *distinctive faith*. It's a very simple idea which requires people of different faiths to identify the distinctive characteristics of their faiths, to articulate them and be clear about them with one another. It requires respect but not agreement.

Jesus did not make any aspect of his ministry conditional. People did not have to change before he served their needs. He served them regardless of who they were or whence they came. The key to Jesus' ministry was that *his* identity did not change. He knew who he was and what he was about – to bring about the kingdom of God on earth, life in abundance.

To have respect for people and be trusted by people, particularly those whose lifestyles clash with ours, requires us to keep our focus on the needs of others while switching our attention from their lifestyles to our own.

At a national level, *distinctive faith* is different from what we might call 'inter-faith'. Inter-faith is a process of 'dialogue' which has made and continues to make a significant contribution to good relations in seeking common ground between faiths in multi-faith Britain. Inter-faith has contributed significantly to the growth of a multicultural Britain. It acknowledges the existence of faith groups, the common ground between them and the need to promote good relations. Inter-faith has become the acceptable face of faith to the public.

However, inter-faith can leave us in a frustrating place, a place which does not acknowledge that there are differences, often mutually exclusive and irreconcilable, between the faiths.

Distinctive faith, on the other hand, enables people of different faiths to maintain the unique characteristics of their faith while being able to relate to others and the needs of communities other than their own. A society where people with different beliefs live harmoniously only begins to be possible when each faith has the opportunity to be itself. Nothing is a greater threat to good community relations than misconstruing people's identities or homogenising different faith identities as one.

But hang on a minute – this sounds to me like code for saying that while all faiths are different, they are really all equal. I thought the point of this chapter would get me to a place of being able to explain that Christianity is unique in its claim to the truth.

That's true from where we are sitting. But going back to your relationship with your friend, you can never really change that person's view or decision without behaving like an equal partner. Criticising or assuming you are right might achieve domination but it rarely, if ever, achieves influence which leads to positive change. If we fail to treat people of different faiths equally and with respect, we stand little or no chance of being heard as Christians, never mind being a good advert for the Christian faith. Yes, it's risky, but being a Christian was never meant to be easy.

I know it sounds odd, but identity is the route to diversity. For good reasons, in the last few years we have witnessed a great rush to embrace others and their differences. Society would have us believe that the route to successful cohesion and integration is the ability to relate to many aspects of multiculturalism in our communities and to get on with everyone. But this approach, as we know, has left us in a muddle, not knowing what we think about one person's difference against another's: veils and crosses, to quote two recent examples, never mind faith schools. What one person considers a right, another considers an offence.

So run that by me again – you are saying that identity solves the difficulties of difference?

Yes. . . once you know who you are and why you think what you think, you are not threatened by another person's identity or fearful of losing yours. You might not agree with that person but whatever he/she thinks or believes is not going to reduce your own identity.

Jesus was unambiguously clear and confident about who he was, where he had come from and where he was going – that's why, despite the protestations of some of the disciples at times and the Pharisees all of the time, he could mix with anyone and run no risk of ever losing his identity as the Son of God. No one could take that from him.

It's the same with us but we need to know our identity, own it and be able not just to believe it but to behave it. So if ever there was a time for us to be clear about our difference as people of faith and to reclaim our identity as Christians, it is now. It is a time to have a separate and distinct identity but in such a way that it overcomes separatism and division. Our distinctiveness has to be robust enough to be able to embrace diversity. Our identity has to be inclusive.

The question we need to address is simply this: what is our identity as Christians and what makes us different?

I have been asking this question for years now, in seminars and workshops looking at what makes Christians and, in particular, Christian social action different from the work of other agencies. Very often the first answer will be that Christian projects are different because they are committed to the poor and the marginalised. So how, I cannot resist asking, do you regard thousands of similar projects undertaken by those who do not consider themselves to be Christians? Are they less good and do they do work of poorer quality? I don't think so. Let's face it, Christians do not have a monopoly on good works.

The next answer with which people come up every time is our theology and the Bible. Yes, the theology of the Christian faith is different from the theology of other religions but the vast majority of the world will only know that it is different when it affects how we behave. The hard fact for some of us to come to terms with is that, despite our own understanding that Christianity has a unique claim to the truth, Christian theology is, in 21st century Britain, just another world view.

What makes us different is not simply what we believe but how our beliefs motivate and affect our behaviour. What makes us different is how our faith transforms the way we live. The difference that the Christian faith has to offer the world today is that Jesus is the full expression of God. The Christian faith is far more than a book of rules. It's a relationship with the living God.

But today, in the 21st century, faith itself is under enormous scrutiny and the Christian faith is just one of nine major faiths in the UK. Unless we accept this and learn to demonstrate the dynamic and transforming relationship between our beliefs and our behaviour, we are in no better position than any other faith. This is the best opportunity we could ever have asked for and it's the riskiest.

So what is distinctive about our faith?

What follows is a short exercise which looks at some of our beliefs, what they mean in everyday language and how they translate into behaviour.

Some core beliefs:

- God is the Creator God
- God is God incarnate in Christ
- God is a redeeming God
- God is a God of grace
- God is the God of resurrection and eternal life
- God is a covenant God
- God is a triune God

Next, what do these beliefs mean?

- *God is the Creator of all people* – God made us all equal and all different
- *God is an incarnational God* – he relates to us as humans through Jesus, whom God sent to help us relate to him and to others
- *God is a redeeming God* – there is no situation which cannot be transformed by God's power and unconditional love demonstrated by the death of Jesus on the cross

- *God is a God of Grace* – God sees the best in us despite our weaknesses and failings
- *God is a resurrection God and God of eternal life* – there is hope, even in death; death is not the end
- *God is a covenant God* – God makes and keeps promises
- *God is a triune God* – God exists in community and he designed us to live and work in relationships

And how do these beliefs translate into our everyday behaviour?

- *God is the Creator all people.* We need to treat all people equally and at the same time, respect their differences.
- *Incarnational God.* As God sent Jesus to help us relate to him, God is interested in how we relate to others and those whom we serve.
- *Redeeming God.* No matter how bad things get, God never gives up on us and he does not want us to give up on others. Even if the funding runs out, we are here for the long term.
- *God of Grace.* God enables us to forgive ourselves and others; it is possible to face difficulties openly and honestly.
- *God of resurrection and eternal life.* We have grounds for hope, even after death. God wants us to be agents of hope – of change and transformation, in our work and in our relationships.
- *Covenant God.* In the same way that God keeps his promises, he wants us to be people of our word – integrity and authenticity are hallmarks of our lives.
- *Triune God.* A strong, caring community should be the focus and aim of the work we do.

Based on the above list of core beliefs, it would therefore be fair to say that the following are some of the *distinctives* of the Christian faith:

- Commitment to people and relationships
- Being inclusive and respecting all people
- Being open and honest when facing conflict
- A hopeful attitude and transforming work
- Integrity and authenticity, keeping promises
- Creating community

And there are many more core beliefs than these and many more distinctive characteristics of the Christian faith but arguing simply about beliefs rarely convinces people of the validity of them. Seeing them in action makes the difference.

Distinctive faith is not a formula which automatically sets the Christian faith over and above other faiths. It is a formula which gives every faith the opportunity to set out what makes it different from other faiths. It is therefore a formula which enables the Christian faith to demonstrate its uniqueness. Jesus did not argue with the rulers of his time about the validity of the kingdom of God; he went about demonstrating the kingdom of God and explaining how to understand it and live it. We have the same opportunity.

DISTINCTLY WELCOMING TIPS

- know your story: keep faithful to your identity as a Christian.
- walk the talk! What behaviour stays true to this story?
- be comfortable and confident with difference: disagreement is a part and parcel of any relationship of quality.
- remind yourself of what behaviour informs our approach to handling difference and disagreement as Christians.
- non-Christians are able to share many of the behaviours and values that we would espouse as Christians. Ensure that you can explain the Christian underpinnings of our values and behaviours when necessary.
- step back from your family arrangements, spending patterns and time management and analyse the priorities. What do you *really* believe in?

A LA CARTE 🍽️ – Luke 9:28–56

Talk about the highs and the lows. One minute, we're there up this mountain and Jesus is lit up like a beacon with two of our dead heroes either side of him. The next minute, we're acting like amateurs faced with a routine deliverance job, squabbling among ourselves about who is the greatest and ready to nuke a Samaritan village. Needless to say, Jesus was less than pleased with how we'd translated the privilege of the mountain into the realities of the valley.

Anyway, I'm running ahead of myself. The mountain business. What you might call a genuine mountain-top experience. It's all beaming lights, booming voices and a glimpse into the next world. A close encounter of the God kind. And, should we have had any doubts, Jesus is most definitely the God kind. That big voice, same as before when Jesus was baptised, 'This is my Son, whom I have chosen; listen to him.' No ventriloquism: God speaking. And the 'Son' is the man we've spent the last three years hanging around; our rabbi, Jesus.

There's this focus about Jesus. You can tell when he's ' in the zone'. You know, like a good batsman. Head still; eyes concentrated, nothing distracting or getting in the way, every action a natural and fluid part of who he is. Well, Jesus seems headed for Jerusalem. We know that means a big bust-up. Not everyone likes him, we know. But we've seen what power is on his side; what strength he can draw from. I reckon we've backed the right horse because no Romans, no dodgy Pharisee leaders will resist Jesus, God's Son. Can you imagine Moses and Elijah and what they would do to the powers-that-be in Jerusalem? All we need now is a replay of the mountain-top scene at Jaffa Gate: Moses on one side, sending a plague on Pilate, that modern-day Pharaoh; Elijah on the other, burning up all the Romans and every last Jew who has compromised and taken the pagan shilling.

So, as disciples, we want to be right in on the action. Who knows what positions might come available when Jesus establishes the new kingdom? We have this debate, you see. Who is the best public speaker and might be Jesus' spokesperson when he confronts Pilate? Or the most holy? You know, most moral, who reads his Torah and prays most frequently. Jesus has to have a good priest around him, surely. And maybe Jesus needs a general. OK, Peter is the obvious choice, all that body-building he does, but a bit of strategy and managerial thinking wouldn't come amiss. But Jesus does his nut. It seems that's irrelevant to his new kingdom. (I'm glad I hadn't had chance to offer my suggestion: Jesus would need a handsome leader to be the public face of a movement that would change the powers in Jerusalem!)

Apparently, all that we think of as the greatest, as the most able, the successful and important, would be reversed. Those who had nothing were rejected, last in the queue, bottom of the pile, in the reject list, second reserve for the second XI, afterthoughts and leftovers, would be at the front, lauded and the greatest. It would all be about serving: doing what he did.

I still don't get it. We end up having to walk through a Samaritan village. The 'enemy', the followers of that competition religion on our doorstep, the unclean among us. We ask for permission to walk through their village. They'd probably kill us if we didn't ask and it sticks in the *throat to ask anything of them. But we do and we get short shrift. 'Take a hike!', they say. 'Take your rabbi somewhere else. You'll just have to take the long way round!' James and John come back with the bad news and they have a great suggestion. 'Hey, Jesus! Shall we send in the angelic F15's on them? Wipe them off the face of the earth?' They'd been reading up on Elijah since seeing him on the mountain. It seems Elijah had done exactly that to the King of Samaria when he'd rejected God's prophet. James and John know their stuff, I'll admit that.*

But Jesus, I still don't get him. He gives them both a real dressing-down, muttering all the while about 'calling', 'service', 'love', 'rejection'. And he gets the 'in the zone' look again. Just where is this guy going and how?

SOUNDTRACK 🎧

Father God, I see myself so much in the disciples. I want to follow you, for I know that Jesus is special and unique. But often it comes out all wrong. I miss your heart, even when I know the right verses, pray the right prayers. Deep down, I know that I am, that we all, are, like children who know nothing. And when we recognise that, you can use us the most. Lord God, give me a picture of who you have called me to be.. May my actions and words flow from a discovery of your love in my life! And help me, because I know that that love leads to sacrifice, costly giving and the cross. Thank you that this is the way to new life and resurrection.

In the name of the King of Kings who became the Suffering Servant. Amen.

TAKEAWAY 🏍

Look at the distinctive faith beliefs which have been suggested. Look at what they mean and how they may translate into everyday life. There are seven for you to consider. Take one distinctive faith belief for each day of this coming week. Meditate in turn on these aspects of faith, starting with 'God is the Creator God'. Chew over each of these beliefs during the day, asking God to show you what these may mean in your work life, family and friendships, and in your church and its ministries. What does it mean for God to be the Creator of all, committed to people and relationships? Use this series of meditations as prayers for guidance and insight. Reflect on daily encouragements and challenges.

BANQUET ⛺
Lesslie Newbigin *The Gospel in a Pluralist Society* (Eerdmans, 1989)

HEALTHY APPETISERS
Andrew Wingate *Celebrating Difference, Staying Faithful* (Darton, Longman & Todd, 2005)

VIRTUAL FOOD
Faithworks: http://www.faithworks.info/index.asp
The Faithworks Charter can be downloaded, with a number of other useful documents providing thinking on *distinctive faith* and society. Information on training and courses is available at www.faithworks.info/training

Chapter 4

Telling it Like it is: Evangelism in a Multi-faith Context

'Knowledge speaks but wisdom listens'.   Jimi Hendrix

There is a guy in our city who stands on a soap-box every Saturday, preaching to shoppers. He has a little group around him, a kind of 'rent-a-crowd', listening. And then there are one or two with leaflets and tracts, poised to accost anyone who looks vaguely interested in what the preacher is saying. I've got to hand it to him: he's brave. That preacher must get loads of abuse but he's there, without fail, Saturday afternoon, ready to make someone's day a misery or a joy, depending on how you look at it.

Once I was walking by that man with my children and my four-year-old, Dylan, pulled my arm down.

'Daddy, why is that man shouting?' Kids are great with questions to make grown-ups squirm. I have to be honest, I always feel guilty walking past that preacher. Half of me is thinking, 'That is just so out of touch; what a bad image he's giving Christians. All that turn and burn stuff!' The other half of me is thinking, 'Well, at least he's being obedient; he's doing evangelism, he's committed and what am I doing except going shopping with my kids?'

I don't know whether, like me, you've ever had ambiguous thoughts about evangelism. What is it that sometimes makes us uncomfortable or embarrassed? We've looked at the key distinctive of the Christian faith: a God of relationship, of love. This book is going to keep hammering away at that theme because this isn't just a neat idea. It's the heart of the Christian faith and should shape everything about us. It means that evangelism is still OK: sharing good news with others is right and proper.

Having discovered the joy of God forgiving us and the wonderful reality of a relationship with him through what Jesus, not we ourselves, has done, it makes utter sense to want others to hear about this. That's part of what it means to be in a relationship; bringing all of who we are, our story and our hopes, into the encounter with others.

There's another side to relationships, too, and that's about listening. If you've ever done any training on communication, the chances are that one element of that communication training has been about the vital component of listening. It's no good talking to people when our words make no sense to them. And we won't know whether our words make sense to them without standing in their shoes. If we think we are saying one thing and the other person is hearing something else and we continue hammering away, we might as well be shouting at them. It's like the sad image of the Englishman in France, struggling with GCSE French to ask for directions from a local. The Gallic blank stare and shrug of the shoulders leads the lost foreigner to speak in English, this time gesticulating and turning the volume up to 'very loud'.

This is the kind of evangelism I often see when Christians communicate with those of other faiths. 'Just speak more loudly!' Now what I want to suggest is not a quick route to success. And throughout the book, there is another consistent theme which I must own right now. I have a confession to make; it might be a little late; but better late than never. If you bought this book looking for the magic secret to filling your church with people from other faiths, then marketing folk probably did their job just a little too zealously. Draw a deep breath, prepare yourself, sit down if you aren't already sitting. *Following Jesus isn't about being successful.* I'm going to have to say that again because even from here, I can sense the cogs whirring, the antennae pricking at the potential heresy. I'm serious. Following Jesus isn't about being successful. Let me unpack this just a little, because we will come back to this point.

When I talk about listening as a component of evangelism, absolutely integral to sharing our faith with people who follow another faith, it isn't primarily that we become more skilled and adept. I do believe that as we listen, we have a better chance of people *hearing* us, and that is bound to pay dividends all round.

But there are no guarantees. No, the first and foremost reason to listen is to be obedient to the pattern of Jesus. Obedience, not success. And, yes, that is counter-cultural. It goes against the grain, even, dare I say it, in our churches.

It goes back again to the Trinity. God, the God *who hears* the cries of his people and sends his Son. The God who didn't stay enthroned as King but who took on human form, lived like us, felt like us, entered into our neighbourhoods and shared our struggles, is our model. Not many of us are kings or have much power to give up but we are called to be like Christ in relationships. That means some journeying, empathising, listening, learning. The Catholic writer Ian Petit describes the young Jesus, apprentice to his dad in the carpentry business. Petit speculates on what Jesus, the Word who was there as stars were flung into space, would have said as Joseph taught him how to saw along the grain of the wood. 'Now hold on, Dad. I designed this. Spare me the rough guide to hardwood. I was the one that came up with the idea of the rings in the trunk measuring the age of the tree!' No. Jesus came as a human and learnt in vulnerability and weakness who he was, his purpose and identity in the Father heart of God. This is what we mean by the incarnation. It's not a concept that is just confined to Christmas. The incarnation is an indicator of what God is like: journeying, identifying, empathising, listening.

An emphasis on the theme of hospitality gets it half right because hospitality in God's economy also requires us to be guests. Jesus, our Lord and King, didn't aspire to being first in the queue, the person who took all the attention, got his own way, shouted the loudest, won all the arguments. Jesus, after the heart of the Father God, welcomed us into his kingdom by being a guest among us. God is both host and guest. So we might have misled you on the title, too. Being distinctive means that sometimes we need to be distinctly welcom*ed*. That is, be prepared to let others be hosts.

During our time in North Africa, my wife and I had to get used to the typical eastern cultural *mores* of hospitality as we settled into the neighbourhood. Here in Britain, our pattern of hospitality would be an invitation to dinner on a Friday night. You know the scene: 'Come along, around 8pm. No need to bring anything. . . well, maybe a bottle of wine'. By this, we are opening our home, affirming people, suggesting we want to get to know them better, expressing some generosity. In eastern cultures, and this is the culture of the Bible, hospitality is expressed in reverse: you show up for dinner unannounced! It takes something for a middle class Brit to get used to this. I have memories of my wife and I steeling ourselves before 'popping in' on neighbours. By doing this, we were giving them respect, showing them generosity, even though we would be guaranteed a huge meal, sometimes at the cost of the hosts' share.

Later we will look at the story in John 4 of the woman at the well, where Jesus, in effect, is doing the same. Across huge cultural, religious and racial barriers, Jesus asks the woman for a drink, deigns to share what she has, even though all the rules suggested that Jesus would be unclean by doing so. Another example is Jesus inviting himself over to Zacchaeus, the tax collector, for dinner. We read this from our western cultural perspective and see Jesus being a little too forward or perhaps compensating for the isolation of the lonely reject. What Jesus was in fact doing was giving public notice of his respect and affirmation of the marginalised tax collector. Jesus' subtext to Zacchaeus and the crowd was, 'I like this man. He is worth sharing food with and I do not care if my reputation is damaged because I am doing this'.

So what does 'being a guest' mean for evangelism? I think it means we need to give space to hear people. I hesitate to use the word 'dialogue' because, especially in a multi-faith context, that carries with it so many other connotations. But it means that evangelism ought not to be a one-way street where 'we' do all the talking and 'they' do all the listening. I believe this is a crucial principle wherever and with whomever we are sharing the good news of Jesus. When it comes to talking with people who have a different faith, this principle just comes into sharper relief. It's like the Jewish rabbi who said, 'Jesus is the answer to a question I never asked.' Many of us are, metaphorically, just turning up the volume when we simply say 'Jesus is Lord' to a person of another faith. We might know Jesus as 'the answer', but that answer simply cannot begin to be understood without our knowing what questions the other person is asking.

For instance, speaking with a Muslim and saying, 'Do you know that Jesus is the Son of God?' may make complete sense to us as Christians. For many Muslims, they are actually hearing, 'This

Christian thinks that God had sexual relations with Mary'!' Saying to a Hindu, 'I believe Jesus is the Son of God.' may precipitate the reply, 'Great! So do I! I have a cross in my room alongside a number of statues that I also believe are sons of God.' A genuine expression of what Jesus means to us in a way that can be heard by someone from another faith requires us to know something about what that person believes; we need to make connections before we can present our challenges.

Can I stop you there? Sure: after all, I have to listen to communicate don't I!

This all sounds a bit intimidating. Are you saying that I can't really do evangelism until I know all the ins and outs of someone else's religion? Because if that's the case, I might as well not bother.

Absolutely not . . . First of all, I believe that sharing about your faith in a manner that involves listening and taking time to understand the other *is* evangelism. Of course, there are times when we might be called on to just be that voice that presents the truth. A whole lot of other people will have done the hard work and the Holy Spirit will have prepared someone's heart and you're just coming in with the right words at the right time. A bit like Philip and the Ethiopian eunuch. You know the story: Philip overhears this Ethiopian reading from the scroll of Isaiah the prophet about a servant leader who would be killed like a lamb slaughtered. There's little time for a relationship and, sure he's done some listening, but basically, it's in with the good news of Jesus being that perfect leader.

. . .OK, you've made your point. But you've not answered my question about having to know so much about other faiths.

Oh yes. I was getting there. You'll have to bear with me, you know. I'm a preacher at heart and once I get going, well you know. No, you don't have to be any kind of expert. Half the battle is approaching with a spirit of humility and inquiry. As I said in the introduction, I would love it if people would go away, after reading this book, determined to find out more about the faiths of people around them. But a genuine spirit of learning and a determination to listen goes a long way. Let's face it: people from another faith don't expect you to know all about their religion. They do expect to be listened to and respected though. I believe they don't want their needs presumed either. What *are* their felt-needs? Many people derive a great comfort from their faith, their prayers and their texts. Do we take time to find out what they are looking and searching for? It's about encouraging evangelism as a conversation.

The classic text for mission is Acts 17 and Paul's sermon at the Areopagus in Athens. It's the story which all the classic weighty tomes on the theology of mission dissect. It's a great model of evangelism which shows Paul making connections and bringing challenges. Maybe you want to conjure up images of the Acropolis in Greece, imagining it intact and bustling with traders and worshippers, not tourists. This was a hub of commerce, culture and religion. For Paul, an observant Jew who had discovered Jesus as his Messiah, it would have been a deeply offensive place: all those statues, all those graven images of gods and goddesses, many representing lewd fertility cults and all a deep affront to any God-fearing Jew.

The account in Acts hints at Paul's inner disturbance as he witnesses the scenes in the city. We get a picture of Paul walking around the city, starting with those places where he is most comfortable – the synagogues. He takes time sharing about Jesus in the familiar context of Jewish worship then in the market-place, the forum for the trade of ideas as well as goods. It seems that Athens enjoyed the latest fad; there was plenty going on and plenty of choice. In that city, you could have your religion latté, decaffeinated, with soya milk or full-fat. How on earth does Paul get the message across in a city with so many competing claims to faith?

Some of the locals are intrigued by what Paul has to say and drag him along to the religious heartbeat of the city: the place with all the best statues, all the religions that count; well, at least those that have had some worthwhile money behind them. So, deep breath, here we go, Paul, follower of the one God, Yahweh, deliverer of

Israel, before whom no other god should be worshipped and no graven idol made, now is your chance.

'People of Athens! I see that in every way you are very religious.' Gulp. Paul is starting with respect. He has been listening and watching. He points to an altar, *To an unknown god*, and begins to tell them about the God of Israel, but not in terms of Israel's history. He talks of the God he knows in terms understandable to the Athenian merchants and philosophers. This 'unknown God' is known to Paul, and Paul has encountered him as a man named Jesus who died and was resurrected.

Interestingly, in this sermon, Paul makes connections to three specific beliefs among the Greeks, finding something in common with them then challenging them, even by quoting one of their own philosophers. To the Stoics who believed that God was in every living thing and experienced in every event, Paul affirms that God can be seen and acknowledged in the life of the Creation. But then Paul challenges them by stressing that God is apart from his Creation. To the Epicureans who believed that God was far from Creation and unconcerned with the day-to-day realities of the planet, Paul affirms that God should not be confused with his Creation. Then he challenges them by telling them how God came and lived among us and is concerned to bring about a new order in which his life would be among us. To the Academics who were cynical of the myths and beliefs of religions because it was impossible to know truth, Paul affirms that there are ridiculous claims made for things made by human hand. But he announces that God can be known and has been revealed and the times of ignorance and separation to which the Academics refer are now over.

It's a blueprint for our evangelism because Paul has clearly done some serious homework with that spirit of inquiry: is there something of God already here? What bridges and connections are ready for the challenge of the good news? Underlying this approach, which effectively creates evangelism as a *conversation* with another world view, is the fact that Paul's message points to concrete realities which the Athenians can test out and verify. Paul's theological and philosophical ideas were not just ideas but explanations of lived-out and tangible experiences: the fact that Jesus, who lived, was crucified and is resurrected; the fact that this community of followers of Jesus who can attest to this news are here in the city, sharing a vibrant new life as a diverse group full

61

of God's Holy Spirit. Ultimately, Paul's words pointed back to what Jesus had done and forward to a community that was modelling this life as an enticing hope in its midst. The hardest and most significant part of evangelism is being the examples and illustrations of the verbal message we share.

The great Christian missionary-scholar Lesslie Newbigin talked of the church's being 'the hermeneutic of the gospel'. This is intellectual shorthand for saying, 'If you want to understand what the gospel is about, look at the church and you will get a big clue'. Evangelism has a place in a multi-faith society when it is infused with a spirit of listening, dialogue and inquiry. Whether we have the luxury of being able to evangelise without expressing practically something of the good news we talk about is another question altogether and one which I will address in our next chapter.

In the meantime, here are a few pointers, in summary, towards the kind of evangelism that may not always be successful but might help us be faithful in a pick-n-mix world of religions and competing claims to the good life:

DISTINCTLY WELCOMING TIPS

- *respecting* – affirm the good in the faith of those you see around you.
- *being humble* – be willing to be a guest; to listen and understand their concerns first.
- *having a spirit of inquiry* – what do they believe? How do they pray? What practices and texts are important to them?
- *making connections* – is there an 'altar to the unknown God' in something of their faith and practice? Find something in their text or belief system which can be affirmed by the Christian faith.
- *making challenges* – at what point do you make a departure and express something of the discomfort of the good news of Jesus?
- *pointing to experiences and realities* – where can your friends and neighbours find practical illustrations of the good news you talk about?
- *being a witness* – be yourself. Share your story. What has God done for you? You don't need to be slick or expert. Just be real and authentic.

A LA CARTE 🍽️ – JESUS AND THE SAMARITAN WOMAN (JOHN 4:1–42)

Dear Jeremiah

A lot has happened since I last wrote to you. I know that you had your doubts about Jesus. Remember: you reckoned that this chippie from the armpit of the north was never going to save our country. Well, I'm wondering whether you are right after all. . . It's not like Jesus isn't making waves, and people certainly want a piece of him. I've been baptising people like there's no tomorrow but I get the impression he has a different agenda from ours.

We've always talked about the need to go back to our roots, follow God more seriously, not compromise with the Romans and we'll be great again. Well, I reckon Jesus is the man if we're talking about serious servants of God. . . and there's not an ounce of compromise in him. But Israel being great and pure. . . I'm not so sure.

Take the other day; it was the usual nervous trek through Samaritan country as Jesus was heading back up to Galilee. You know what it's like in Samaria these days: they'd sooner rob you than look at you. It's bad enough having these idol-worshipping Romans running the country but having to live cheek by jowl with the half-breed Samaritans is just the final insult. God is either punishing us big-time or just doesn't care anymore. Anyway, needless to say, we were all a bit jittery. For a big bloke, my mate Peter doesn't half get wound up around Samaritans and we were all a bit tense, to be honest. So we stocked up on food and water, making sure we wouldn't break the regulations by sharing their foul stuff. It's noon and the sun is cracking the flags cos we were hoping that no-one would be around, all those cross-breeds tucked up for a siesta doubtless plotting their schemes or worshipping whatever gods they worship.

It was blistering hot. We wanted to get through there quickly. I didn't want to be like those pilgrims a few years back who came a cropper and were knifed to death on their way to Jerusalem. We were all gagging for a drink, all water gone, and Jesus seemed even more weary than us. So he stopped for a rest while we went off to rustle up some packed lunches from somewhere. This Samarian business so depresses me. . .We were at Sychar, you know, the land that Jacob gave to Joseph. That was our place; our holy site. To think of the humiliation of Samaritans owning it now! Jacob would turn in his grave.

We rounded the corner and right ahead, in the centre of the village, was Jesus. I couldn't believe it! We'd planned to trot through the town sharpish. . .no hanging about. But there he was, the northern carpenter. . .

63

supposed saviour of Israel, talking with a Samaritan woman next to the town well!

Now you're not stupid, Jeremiah, I know. You might be miserable like your name-sake but you can put two and two together. . .what's a self-respecting woman doing, even if she is a Samaritan, drawing water from a well at mid-day, you may ask? Clearly, she wasn't a self-respecting woman! Even those degenerate Samaritans had some sense of propriety and gave her a wide berth. Between you and me, Jeremiah, she wasn't half pleasing on the eye, but you can't have a project to save Israel and bring back the good old days and start consorting with women like that!

John writes a diary and he showed me what he wrote about this earlier. He said that none of us dared ask Jesus why he was talking to the woman. That was the question going through all our heads, right enough. We're all raising our eyebrows at each other; just a little too uncomfortable with whatever has gone on here. To cap it all, Jesus and the woman are both grinning away like they've just shared a joke and Jesus is drinking her water. I try and remember that hundreds of years before, Jacob would have drunk from this same well and it would be OK, but it doesn't work. Jesus, the supposed saviour, seems somehow contaminated now.

It was weird, I tell you. Jesus is a really tactile bloke; loves a hug, and I'll be honest, makes us disciples feel like a million dollars normally. But he was now unclean. Technically, we disciples should have run a mile from him, but we couldn't. He just drew us into all that was happening and it felt like it was God-business. But we were in new territory here, though. This woman started waking up all her neighbours from their siestas, telling them about Jesus. And we were right; she did have a che-quered history. Peter said she counted all her, quote, 'husbands', and she didn't even know the name of the chump that was in her house right then sleeping it all off. It was quite a sight. . .We disciples, getting more nervous by the minute as Samaritans were appearing as this woman, like some town crier, roused the whole town, saying how wonderful Jesus was and how he was the answer to all their problems.

This following Jesus lark was getting rather complicated. I got the low-down from the others later. It seems he'd made a bee-line for her when we'd have all gone in the opposite direction, and actually asked her for a drink! Can you believe it? He seemed to know all about her, understood where she was coming from, was interested in her and even quoted some of what the Samaritans believed.

Now since I've been part of Jesus' crew, I've enjoyed the way that he involves us. We're the ones doing all the baptising; he's even got us doing healings and teaching. We all know that Jesus is the one making it happen but we get to play a part and that feels good. Just to cap it all with this dodgy Samaritan woman, she's telling her town how Jesus is the bees' knees and we end up staying two nights. Within 48 hours, there's this new band of Jesus disciples carrying on his message in the heart of heathen-land. I don't know how Jesus hopes to keep it on the straight and narrow and it's not going to help his reputation in Jerusalem with the religious bigwigs.

Don't tell a soul, but, as you probably gathered, we had to drink their water, eat their food, share their plates. I really don't know what's going on. Jesus is certainly someone special but when women with histories like hers from tribes like the Samaritans suddenly get a piece of God, I wonder where it will all end.

SOUNDTRACK 🎧

Evangelism can be so incredibly daunting and guilt-inducing. I suspect we all carry our own baggage of what evangelism means to us and perhaps some very negative experiences of it. Take this time to be real about this with God. If you feel diffident and afraid, own that and share that with God. If you feel stricken with guilt that you're embarrassed to speak publicly about your faith, tell God about that. too. If evangelism is your scene but you feel uncomfortable with some of this chapter, perhaps the making of connections with another faith or the willingness to be a guest, then take that to God, too. God is patient and kind and even published Christian books get things wrong; so pray a prayer for guidance and help. Ask God for strength and confidence in your own witness, that you would be true to him and true to yourself.

TAKEAWAY 🏍

Do some research, a little like Paul in Athens! Prayerfully consider one friend or neighbour of another faith. If you can't think of anyone of another specific faith, then consider someone you know who is an atheist or spiritual searcher, perhaps exploring New Age spiritualities. Find out one thing about what the person believes or does as part of religious practice or a text the person reads with which you can make a connection. Find something that you as a Christian can agree with and affirm that may even point to Jesus in some way. Pray for the person and ask God to give you an opportunity to find out more personally about what he/she believes. Pray for the chance to respond naturally with both similarities and differences about what Jesus means to you.

BANQUET 🏠
Richard Bauckham *Bible and Mission: Christian Witness in a Post-modern World* (Paternoster Press, 2003)

HEALTHY APPETISERS 🍎
Ida Glaser and Shaylesh Raja *Sharing the Salt*, a gentle introduction and encouragement to engagement with people of different faiths, published by Scripture Union, ISBN 1 85999 307 9, copies still available from Kitab Oriental Books, Satis@kitab.org.uk

See info@southasianconcern.org for the following resources:
The New People Next Door: insights, suggestions and study resources for those communicating with people from a South Asian background.
Looking for Directions – towards an Asian Spirituality: exploring South Asian spirituality in the modern world.
Masala Bridge Builders and Discovery Groups: materials and ideas for small group discussions on issues of concern to South Asians on the Christian life.
East+West Asian Equip: course giving training that leads to the development of good relationships and appropriate sharing of the Christian faith with South Asian neighbours.

See www.scriptureunion.org.uk for *Jesus in the Bible/What is a Christian?/The Christian View of the Bible* – leaflets explaining Christian truths in a way which engages a Muslim world-view.

VIRTUAL FOOD 🖱
See www.cocm.org.uk for resources available for understanding and communicating with Chinese groups in the UK.
Urban Vision: http://www.interserveonline.org.uk/urbanvision. htmfor support and resources for cross-cultural UK mission.
http://www.kitab.org.uk for literature resources for communication with Muslims.
www.globalconnections.co.uk/findresources/ – a network resource for diverse mission issues.
www.faithtofaith.org.uk for any inquiries on materials, networks and courses on communicating with people of other faiths.

Chapter 5

Serving with Distinction
Community Action and other
Faiths

'We may be poor, but we're laughing all the way to the banquet'.
Andrew Jones

Over the last 20 years, it seems that much of the church in Britain
has rediscovered its calling to work alongside the poor and vulnerable and to recognise the component of justice in the good news
Jesus brings. Certainly those of us from an evangelical tradition
are more readily concerned to see issues such as international
trade, the sex trade and community regeneration as arenas to bring
kingdom transformation. I'm not going to tread old ground on
definitions of mission but rather simply to reassert that when Jesus
died on the cross, the power of sin over believers was broken and
a new creation inaugurated. From now until Jesus' return, the
church is in the vanguard of a new life of forgiveness, justice, righteousness and wholeness towards which we work in faith and
hope. One day soon, even the environment will enjoy complete
renewal!

It's a grand vision and one that is inspiring Christians across
Britain to serve in debt advice centres, homeless hostels, environmental projects, asylum seeker befriending, children's nurseries
and employment training projects. While I was growing up in a
vicarage, in what you might call a 'true-blue' evangelical household, I used to hear the phrase 'social gospel'. I realised that 'social
gospel' was not a compliment. The argument went something like
this: the 'social gospel' churches neglected things such as Bible
study, prayer and preaching. In fact, preaching in social gospel
churches was apparently just a political message, and that would
only last for five minutes anyway, not like the twenty-five minute
sermons of exposition in a proper church! What was the *point* of

doing social action when the council was likely to be better at it than us? Social gospellers had forgotten what church was *really* about. Not only that, but worse. They had traded in the grace and freedom of Christ for working hard at their salvation, trying to impress God with good works.

I'm exaggerating and caricaturing but you get the idea. Thankfully, this sort of attitude is less common now, and churches from a huge range of traditions are committing themselves to tackling issues of poverty, whether locally or in the international arena, through organisations such as Tear Fund and Christian Aid. But may I stop there and just throw a spanner in the works? I do think there is a valid criticism in some of these attitudes. As I write these words, I can hear the sharp intake of breath from where you are sitting, even in my office here in Birmingham! I'm conscious that this kind of book is in danger of alienating everyone: evangelicals who don't think I am recommending a hard enough line on other faiths and liberals who think I talk too much about the Bible and still advocate evangelism. But here goes, in for a penny, in for a pound. . . I wonder sometimes whether churches committed to community projects forget who they are. So often the Christian motivation and fuel gets lost, with the danger that the project or community involvement becomes just another well-meaning intervention.

I need to explain myself. We've begun to look at the concept of 'distinctive faith' and how knowing our Christian roots and calling is crucial to embracing and engaging with diversity. Christians have a clear text and traditions which inform how they will be and why they should be committed to justice. When we are involved, the challenge is to ensure we know what these beliefs and traditions are and can embody them in practice, not to neuter our faith as we engage in good works.

Let's look at the suggested hallmarks of a distinctive faith again:

- God is the Creator God
- God is God incarnate
- God is a redeeming God
- God is a God of grace
- God is the God of resurrection and eternal life
- God is a covenant God
- God is a triune God

How might these beliefs be translated into the motivations and practices of a church concerned, say, to clear up a neighbourhood full of rubbish and litter, where residents regularly complain of the unpleasant and uncared-for environment?

1. God is the Creator God – the God who looked at Creation and declared it good and called men and women to be stewards of Creation helps us see that this projects flows from the heart of who God is. As the church clears up the neighbourhood, are there fresh and imaginative solutions to the problem, creative partnerships and artistic gifts that can flower in the renewed environment?

2. God is God incarnate – the God who entered our world and felt what we felt challenges us to live in the situation of those we seek to love and serve. Does the church pay for professionals to remove the waste or literally get its hands dirty? How much should we expect and encourage church members to be living amongst those among whom they minister?

3. God is a redeeming God – can any of the waste be recycled or turned into something useful? Have we chosen the easiest neighbourhood to deal with or should there be a declaration of intent to transform the untidiest, messiest street because nothing is beyond God's transformative powers?

4. God is a God of grace – are we doing this work in order to support something we perceive as more important, such as an evangelistic event to which the community will be invited? Or is this gracious, open-handed, unconditional love, without ulterior motive or hidden agendas?

5. God is the God of resurrection and eternal life – how do we give hope to the community that the problem will not just revert to normal once the church has done a clear-up exercise? Are we considering sustainable solutions that offer genuine hope for a future which the community will welcome? Might these solutions be ongoing clear-up projects coupled with strategic conversations with the council and other groups?

6. Covenant God – as God is true to his word, how do we authenticate our promises and stay committed to the community? What might the hallmarks of a trustworthy project be to the community?

7. Triune God – if God is a God of relationship, in what ways do we ensure that this is more than just a 'project' but an inter-action of individuals in relationship? Can the project open up opportunities for friendships, listening and fun across the community?

I hope the above hypothetical exercise gives a little pointer as to how the substance of a church's community involvement is estab-lished from within its own identity, its distinctiveness. The ques-tions, and they have to be questions because the answers will be unique to a time and place, were all framed around the church project's relationship to the community. Equally, we ought to be considering the internal structures of the church or para-church body. So, if God is a covenant God, how do we ensure that staff members are treated with respect and that promises made about pay, for example, are made good? An incarnate God might chal-lenge project hierarchies which remove senior staff from ever having contact with the community the project serves. Or believ-ing in a redeeming God may underpin a decision to be a Fair Trade community which uses recycled paper.

There is huge scope for how our faith informs and shapes the social action projects of churches. As with so much of the material in this book, these principles are also applicable in all our working lives and relationships. I believe that once we begin to think in terms of rooting our practice in the values of the Christian story, the extra dimension of relationship to other faiths becomes clearer.

When I run seminars on relating to other faiths, one of the ques-tions I like to throw out is, 'What do you think is the single most distinctive aspect of Christian belief?' It's a good question because when you're involved in teaching about other religions, you inevitably get bogged down in some of the similarities between peoples and beliefs and it can be quite disorientating and trou-bling. Being called back to a single distinctive is helpful but also a challenge. I get answers such as 'the cross', 'forgiveness' or 'Jesus'. Now plenty of religions could affirm those answers and I think people are nearer the mark when they propose, 'Jesus is Lord' or 'the Trinity'. In one sense, the concept of the Trinity underpins all the hallmarks of our distinctive faith.

The Creator God is the Father, the Eternal Word and the Spirit. We understand God through the incarnation of his Son, and we in turn are called to incarnate the life of Christ through the Spirit. The redeeming nature of God is demonstrated in the cross where death is defeated and where all humanity can turn to obtain new life in the Spirit. God's grace is manifest in the Son, full of grace and truth, full of the Spirit. We can trust in the resurrection of the dead and the newness of all things because the Father raised the Son from death and his Spirit is poured out on believers as a sign and promise of the new creation to come. God's covenant with us is established in the blood of the cross of his Son and sealed in us by the presence of the Spirit. Belief in a 'Triune God' is therefore something more than an abstract and mystifying theology but the kernel of the Christian faith.

Having taken a dangerous side-road into one of the Christian beliefs most designed to baffle and intimidate, it's worth coming back to how this translates specifically into church community projects and interaction with other faiths. Let me share some stories about a church project I know well. Based in an inner city area, the church is in a Muslim-majority district with a significant number of Hindus, Sikhs and white non-Christians. The local mosque faces the church and vicarage and for some years the church has run a nursery and carers and toddlers facility. As the project has grown in success and obtained additional funding, a professional nursery, associated family support, after schools clubs and youth work have been established.

'Let the draught go both ways.'

The project started out as a sub-committee of the church leadership, but as it has grown, the Christian staff and volunteers have been augmented by Muslim, Sikh, Hindu and atheist volunteers and staff. There has always been a clear vision that the project is a vital part of the church's mission. Yet there is this nagging question of how this could be so when non-Christians are involved. For some in the church, there has been the struggle to reconcile a passion for sharing the good news of Jesus with the constraints of professional good practice and equal opportunities legislation. Are these limitations yet more examples of a secular nation squeezing the life out of the church? Should we then see the project as our 'works', with the invariably more significant 'words' seen as something separate?

These have been and continue to be huge questions for the church, and I see them replicated throughout the country. A mindset that comes with a distinctive faith approach will see much of the good professional practice and equal opportunities legislation as things that the church should be publicly upholding as they seek to acknowledge and affirm the diversity of society by the protection of weaker and more vulnerable groups. We may wish to challenge some of the prioritising of the respective minority groups and, as we noted earlier, communicate a better understanding of Christian motivations and values to local and central government. But churches can and should embody fairness and justice not merely as a sop to social obligations but as an authentic expression of who we are.

So back to the nitty-gritty questions of the church in the inner city. . . Could this project, which is prayed for in church services and managed as a sub-committee of the church leadership, have paid senior staff who are Muslims or atheists? The answer I would give is, 'It depends.' Part of the answer relates to the project and its clarity of values. Does it have rooted motivations and practices in the Christian faith and text? If so, then the church is a long way to being more than 'just a social project'. But the other part of the answer relates to the applicants. They may even share many of the values that are translated into practice. They may not share the core beliefs, but if they can affirm the values and practices, why not?

In 1 Kings 17, the prophet Elijah is a refugee in the Sidon region. He's in pagan country and let's not forget that soon after this incident, Elijah is involved in a sight and sound contest with the priests of the false god Baal on Mount Carmel. So Elijah is no woolly liberal. It's interesting that Jesus refers to this story in his own ministry, much to the annoyance of his home synagogue. And God calls Elijah to the home of a widow in a town called Zarephath near Sidon to be fed by her. The woman has nothing but God provides for her family and for Elijah. After some time, the widow's son falls ill and dies and the widow rebukes Elijah as a man of God who has brought this calamity on her because of her sin. Elijah prays for the son and God heals him. The closing statement in the story has the woman declaring, 'Now I know that you are a man of God and that the word of the LORD from your mouth is the truth.'

It's a rich tale and one with particular resonance for a multi-faith context. I see something of Christ in Elijah's willingness to receive from the widow. He was obeying God by allowing himself to be a guest of this adherent of another faith. The reality was that God was providing food for the family, but the relationship was one of equality and exchange, of risk and mutuality. There is no sense of Elijah's begrudgingly obeying by staying with the widow and preaching to her at all hours. Rather, his presence brought blessing, a blessing which he received also, and they became a blessing to each other. With the amazing healing of her son, there is the discovery of the personal relationship with God who is Lord of all. But all that had preceded the healing had been without guile, unconditional, free and authentic and was a foundation for the personal decision the widow eventually made. Elijah could interact on the basis of an equal relationship because he knew God's call on his own life.

So back to the community project. What do Elijah and the widow have to do with community projects and other faiths? Everything! You see, so much of our practical service is about 'doing good works to them.' The 'them' are generally the poor and 'people not like us'. An incarnational faith which recognises that we are all fallen, are all in need of a forgiving, loving God and that all people and situations can be redeemed, will work *with* others in the mission of God, because in genuine relationships the parties are never unchanged. Now we know that God, in one sense, never changes, but he listens to us, he hears us, he is responsive to us. Supremely, in Jesus, God came close to us. The Lord feels what we feel and experiences what we experience. The essence of incarnation is God's accommodation to our lives in order to transform our lives into his life. How can we follow that pattern when we are the blessed and powerful ones, dispensing goods to the lowly down there? It just doesn't fit the Christian story.

So we have Elijah, that frightening prophet, seeking the hospitality and provision of a pagan widow. Elijah is taking a risk and being vulnerable, and so is the widow. Real relationships require risky vulnerability and are charged with unpredictability. Would this woman have any food, would it be right for me, as a Jew, to eat it? Would this prophet use up all my family's food; would he be prophesying about what a sinner I am in my own home? The widow's clear commitment to hospitality became a shared value that brought relationship even in their diversity.

The church nursery project was, for many years, based in the church hall. A draughty corridor-cum-meeting room connected

the church and the hall and became a motif for the church's connection with the community: 'Let the draught go both ways.'
Holding true to our story and to our own identity, a genuine
encounter of service required the church to be changed as it
stepped out in vulnerability. So, would the appointment of non-
Christians who shared the values of the project and worked as
good professionals water down the Christian distinctive of the
project? It might, but prayerful, faithful commitment from the
church, its staff and volunteers has been vital in distinguishing
the project as a truly Christian embodiment of hope within an area
which visitors may see as very alien to Christ. The church hall has
been knocked down and a purpose-built Children's Centre is to
take its place. In the meantime, the nursery, against all received
wisdom for other-faith communities, thrives in the main body of
the church. The many Muslim parents are also stepping out in vulnerability by having to walk through a church entrance (an
entrance, I remind you, opposite the local mosque) and give their
children to the safe keeping of staff and volunteers working in the
shadow of a large cross.

The church would say it has a long way to go, and there are discussions to be had about representation on the management group
of other faith members who have a stake in the services. Here is
another example of likely mutual vulnerability! The tone of this
vulnerability is not doormat Christianity. I am not advocating that
churches throw aside all they hold dear. Rather, our aspiration is
the humility of Christ that knows exactly who he is and what he is
called to do and thus to cling ever more tightly to Christ. His
example will lead us to challenge and speak out against sin and
injustice, but to do so from a life laid down in selfless love.

The big difference between us and Christ, and the added oblig-
ation to humility, is that we mess up. We only know in part. We
also *need* other people and other groups in fulfilling God's mission
on earth. Robert Chambers, a guru in the field of overseas development studies, has pioneered a way of bringing sustainable
change to poorer communities by starting with what the community already knows. Chambers would say that long term transformation will only come when we tap into the resources that
pre-exist well-intentioned outsiders. One of his mantras is 'Pass
the pencil over'! Chambers advocates mapping the key sites in a
village or town, with the associated water sources and fields as a

starting point. He encourages listening to tribal elders, the women, the children, but always, whenever you can, to 'pass the pencil over'. Instead of the development professional drawing the resources map, invite the villagers to do it. When they see their situation for themselves, transformation is more likely to be owned. We can sketch out our view of what *we* see and hear, but we need to give dignity to the voice and experience of the other party. Again, it's the incarnational 'standing in their shoes' approach, modelled by Jesus, which ought to be our pattern.

I believe biblical principles support this motif from the world of development studies. God never colonises us; he never marches in on us, forcing his ways on our will. God doesn't manipulate, control or destroy us. The Trinitarian God loves us, gives us space to be who we are, listens to our heart cries, woos us, gives us dignity, invites us to respond and be a fellow-partner, hears our prayers. This is a real relationship and it's messy and unpredictable. And in this furnace we find out more about who we really are and can become more fully who we are called to be.

MORE THAN WHISPERS

Rooting Christian social action in a concept of distinctive faith puts Christ firmly in the public square. Reflecting on the values of our faith and how they translate into meaningful behaviour and practice is a more potent presence for transformation in society because we are forced to embody our faith in the Christian story. The founder of IKEA, Ingvar Kamprad, uses stories to illustrate the brand of the ubiquitous Swedish flat-pack firm. Kamprad is famous for saying how he always uses public transport: he tells of travelling from the airport to home on a local bus. In that simple story, the wealth and power of IKEA become tempered with a connection to the ordinary person. 'IKEA knows what my life is like'.

Stories have far more authority than dogma and facts. People are enticed by stories, feel a part of stories, see a new vision of the future or a fresh perspective on their past in the telling of tales. And stories hold storytellers to ransom. Kamprad's anecdote suddenly becomes an embarrassment if he is spotted in a stretch limo driving out of Gothenburg airport. It's a lot less potent to hide behind a vision statement which commits a firm to 'understanding its customers' and easier for it to mean nothing. The story gives the bland intention a life of its own.

I believe the church's commitment to community transformation should be a series of storytelling, rooted in our big story of God's purposes for a new creation. It will mean that we explain the reason for the hope we have for the world and be a publicly praying and worshipping community as we engage. It will mean that with humility, we partner other faiths in issues of common concern, being robustly Christian but rejoicing in the grace we find beyond our boundaries. The stories we tell will hold us to ransom about how we treat staff, how we forgive, show mercy, see possibilities for good in every situation and in all people. Oh, and lest we forget, we keep on messing up. So part of our storytelling must be a public acknowledgement that we are just like any other human – frail, sinful and weak. That forgiveness is vital in relationships and available in the God we worship.

If you are involved in an aspect of community transformation or Christian social action, what stories give life to your being rooted in the story of the Bible? Here are some concluding challenges towards a distinctly welcoming project that might embody these stories:

DISTINCTLY WELCOMING TIPS

intentional vulnerability – do you hold all the cards and is it all down to the Christians 'doing it to them'? Or do you make space to be challenged, to learn and work with others?

risky unpredictability – are you always in control and following a set programme and agenda? Or have you the flexibility to be responsive to unanticipated needs and hear the voices of others?

spiritual practicality – do you keep your prayer-life and worship private and individualized? Or do you allow the fuel for your ministry to shape the communal practice and direction of the project? Many of our other-faith communities will respect and welcome prayerful, worshipping Christians even if secular society does not.

biblical accountability – do you apologise for your Christian roots, silencing the source of your motivations and inspirations? Or do you affirm your practice with the roots of Scripture as you engage with other faiths and secular agencies. Remember that presenting the roots of our hope challenges other groups to reflect on what motivates them, too.

In Southall, West London, the Christian environmental mission agency *A Rocha* is engaged in a wonderful conservation project in one of the most built-up and neglected districts in the country. With an explicit Christian charge to bring redemption to a local park, the agency and associated churches are working alongside Muslims, Sikhs and Hindus who share a mandate to be stewards of creation. The work is distinctive, Bible-based, cooperative, and a glorious cameo of what is possible. Is it too much to dream of a million such endeavours of Christ-centred new creation activities across our nation?

A LA CARTE 🍽️ – John 2:1–11

I hate weddings! All this focus on the gorgeous couple, all that hanging around, toasts to Aunt Flossy who can't be here, bad speeches and bad dancing. I never could get what all the crying was about either, unless you count a display of fashion disaster hats as emotional abuse! I guess I have a good reason to hate weddings: I have to go to loads of them. I'm a waiter, and I work for a firm that specialises in doing only the best nuptials celebrations: 'Wedded to quality' is the motto.

I say I hate weddings but we had the most bizarre reception last week. It certainly broke the pattern of what I had come to expect at these events. There we were in Cana, just north of Nazareth. It was all going along swimmingly but after a while my antenna is out; like any good waiter, you have to anticipate, see in advance what the clients need. Anyway, it seems that there's more than a fair share of fishermen and carpenters in this crowd, and they drink like fish! It wasn't a shoestring reception by any means but clearly someone in the family has done the calculations wrong and the wine is fast running out. We waiters are eyeing each other across the tables, taking that extra bit of time before refilling glasses, studiously avoiding the glances of those who are downing their pinot noir just a little too swiftly.

The maitre d' gets wind of what's going on and is like a cat on hot bricks. Highly strung at the best of times, that vein on his forehead bulging with stress. 'Oh, our reputation! What will we do? The families will be publicly humiliated if the wine is finished before the party is over! We'll never do business in Galilee again!!' He sends out one of the young apprentices to search for local wine supplies, but I know Cana's stocks have been cleaned out.

The trouble is, some of the guests start to notice the suppressed panic among the staff and near-empty glasses now dominating the tables. The head of the bridegroom's family would be so shamed if the wine ran out. It's not simply about a nice tipple; it's a symbol of fruitfulness, of God's blessings on us and our own identity as Jews. It goes right back to the Exodus and the spies bringing back those huge clusters of vines from the Promised Land. At a wedding, you just gotta have the wine, or else!

This woman is chatting to one of the other waiters. Mary is her name and I'm beckoned over. It seems she reckons her son is the bees' knees: been there, done that, got the T-shirt. Well, a fair few Jewish mums fit that description, but Mary's quite adamant that her boy will sort out our predicament.

Her boy happens to be this rabbi called Jesus, and he's giving his mum the hard stare. You know the kind I mean: 'Mum, don't embarrass me in public! I don't need you to push me forward, thank you'. It seems he doesn't want to be involved and is 'not ready'. What was all that about? Ready for what? If he's got a secret stash of wine, now is the time to give it up! But Mary is persistent, keeps badgering her boy and just says to us waiters, 'Do anything, I mean anything he says!!' I get the drift: the anything could be something really weird, but, hey, we've nothing to lose.

Jesus takes us to the hallway where the stone water jars are kept. Huge jars these; they hold over 75 litres. 'Fill them'. Simple instruction. . .OK, I can do that. 'Now draw some water out and take it to the maitre d'.' Mmmmm. That's the really weird bit. Have you seen what's in those jars? That's the water we use for washing feet when people arrive. The job you start out on when you join this firm. There's all sorts of stuff in those jars! Our streets are none too clean and our feet, well, we'd rather not talk about them. I breathed a big sigh of relief when I graduated to being a waiter. Not for me that daily acquaintance with a cross between bad cheese and the farmyard. And this rabbi Jesus is for pouring water into wine glasses out of this stuff!

I'm giggling now; that nervous laughter you get that you can't control. Well, in the pecking order I'm one up from Amos so I tell him, 'I'll help you get the water out, you take it over to the maitre d''. Amos is looking at me like I'm mad. 'He'll kill us! We can't serve this stuff!' Jesus gives us that hard stare again. So we go for it. Water in the jars, in all that gunge and dirt. Jugs in, and neither of us dare look at what scummy stuff is being taken to the tables.

I peer around the doorway as Amos carries the first jar over to the maitre d'. He looks like a rabbit caught in headlights. We, and Jesus, are the only ones who know what's really in the jar. Jesus is now just grinning at me. Here is the moment of truth. The maitre d' pours the wine into a glass, and it's a deep red. Maybe someone was bleeding the last time the waters were used for cleaning. My mouth is dry with anticipation as the glass is raised to his lips and he tastes before handing the jug to the head table. 'This wine is amazing! Beautiful!' I see him take the bride-groom aside and say something about how unusual it is to leave the best wine till last.

It's party time now! I'm running around like I'm on casters filling jugs and serving tables. Apparently it's like some Chateau Lafitte vintage. Everyone is loving it; the reception is now really swinging. I spot Jesus with his fishermen mates. He's grinning again, happy that people are happy. Mary and Jesus' followers are the only ones who know who really served us that day. A whole community has been given a great party by this rabbi Jesus, and only a few of the party could tell you who Jesus actually is.

I'd forgotten about me and Amos, though. Yeah, we'd seen what had gone on, what had really transformed that wedding. That day I realised I had some choices of my own to make. That rabbi was something else.

SOUNDTRACK 🎧
Transforming God,
You transform water into wine
Dregs into abundance
A flat reception into a party.

Transforming God,
Transform my efforts into your fruitfulness
My sin into your good life
My sadness into your joy.

Transforming God,
Help me to be an agent of creation, where there is destruction
Wholeness where there is brokenness
Hope where there is despair.

Be a transforming God
In my life
In the church
In my community
In the world
Amen

TAKEAWAY

Are you involved in an aspect of community service, whether with your local church or as an individual volunteer or perhaps even in your employment? How much of what you do flows from your Christian faith and your understanding of the good news of Jesus? How is your own practice both 'distinctive' and 'welcoming'? Write an inventory noting the aspects of motivation and values which are a core part of your community involvement. Note those aspects which can serve the whole community and share common concern and values with those of other faiths and none.

Pray through this inventory, asking God to show you where you need to be more conscious of Christian distinctiveness, or more welcoming of the challenges and learning which are part of a welcoming relationship.

BANQUET

David Bosch *Transforming Mission: Paradigm Shifts in Theology of Mission* (Orbis Books, 1991)

HEALTHY APPETISERS

Malcolm Duncan *Building a Better World: Faith at Work for Change in Society* (Continuum, 2006)

Edited by David Lee *Ministry and Mission in a Multi-Faith Society* (Diocese of Birmingham, 2001). Reflections of a working party in the Diocese of Birmingham; including stories of witness and working alongside neighbours of different faiths. Available from http://www.birmingham.anglican.org.

See www.mph.org.uk for *May I Call You Friend?*, a resource available from The Methodist Church, exploring practical issues around involvement with those of other faiths.

VIRTUAL FOOD

Enabling Christians in Serving Refugees – a web resource and community aiding those working alongside asylum seekers and refugees.
http://www.ecsr.org.uk/cm/general/, including signposts to other agencies, with the *Lifewords* resources on http://lifewords.info/asylum/engage/

Faithworks: http://www.faithworks.info/index.asp for resources and networking of Christian based community projects. For information on training courses and consultancy for Christian community development work, see www.faithworks.info/training

The Micah Challenge: http://micahchallenge.org/english/ information and resources on integral mission and the need for Christians to be active in pursuing justice.

Chapter 6

Young at Heart: Youth and Children's Work

'And just remember, different people have peculiar tastes.
And the glory of love, the glory of love,
The glory of love might see you through'.   Lou Reed

Aside from climate change, arguably the greatest challenge facing the world today is how people of different faiths get along together. Combine this with the perennial paranoia that exists about young people, and there is a heady mix sufficient to put off anyone seeking to engage in youth and children's work across faiths. Religious fanaticism, hoodies, graffiti, child protection and delinquency are enough to set even the most laid back pulses running. However, the reality on the ground is far from the panics and scares we may see in our newspapers. Our young people are far more comfortable with the diversity of Britain than their elders. Not for them the questioning and grief about a vanishing way of life: monoculturalism is dead; long live diversity!

Young people have an unerring knack of asking the insensitive but important question without the guile of their parents. This means that there is massive potential to equip this new generation for the sort of open and understanding relationships between faiths which are so much more difficult when encumbered with the cynicism and reserve of age. A friend of mine does a considerable amount of work bringing together Muslim and Christian young people to remove preconceptions and encourage confidence in relating across the two faiths. On one such occasion, a group of Christian girls plucked up the courage to ask a veiled Muslim teenager, 'Can you tell us how your friends recognise you when you're wearing the veil?' This is dialogue youthful style: an honest and vital question for the

Christian girls, asked in genuine curiosity and answered with equal enthusiasm.

For much of this chapter, I'm going to leave you in the good hands of my friend who is involved in youth work with Christians and Muslims. Andrew Smith heads up a Scripture Union programme called 'Youth Encounter'. Andrew, or 'Smeee' as he is most commonly known, is bringing together years of Christian youth work practice and experience with an unerring grasp of 'distinctive faith'. What follows for most of this chapter is from him.

We will look at the issues surrounding Christian youth and children's work when engaging with other faiths and the nature of Christian presence in schools which present a multi-faith constituency. The material in this chapter cannot hope to cover all the bases in the breadth of youth and children's ministry. Rather, we will highlight some key issues and signpost further resources available for more detailed study.

A DISTINCTLY WELCOMING CHRISTIAN YOUTH AND CHILDREN'S WORK TO THOSE OF OTHER FAITHS

Christian youth and children's work encompasses a whole range of motivations, projects and contexts. Some church-based youth outreach programmes are plainly evangelistic and others are church-based youth projects aimed at equipping youngsters in a climate of neglect. Children's programmes may include exciting holidays built around Bible teaching or a week's entertainment and craft activities as a community service while the local school is shut. Whatever the flavour and substance of a church's engagement with young people and children of other faiths, several common considerations are required.

Let's begin by picturing a scene. Imagine some Muslims from a local mosque decide that they want children in their area to hear about Islam. They set up a team of volunteers (who all have the necessary child protection proofs) to take assemblies and run after-school clubs. Certain volunteers decide to meet regularly with some of the young people who hang out at the local playground and invite them to basketball sessions at a sports centre. They then provide good quality holiday clubs in the hall attached to the mosque during school holidays. The group states that they are Muslims and will teach stories of Mohammed but that they will always respect the faith and culture of any children who come along.

84

Mmm. How would you feel if this started to happen in your area? What if the head teacher welcomed them into the school where your children (or children you know) go? What if those children get an invitation to the club and are desperate to go? What questions would you have for the head teacher or for the Muslims?

Here are some of the feelings and questions you might have owned as I presented this scenario:

Fear: are my children going to be alienated from me and follow a religion I don't share which goes against the clear faith of my family? Are they going to be manipulated into following something extreme which will be in conflict with this family's values?

Suspicion: what are their motivations? Do they have the best interests of my children at heart? Are they even professional in what they have to offer?

Anger: how dare they come and do this here! This is our neighbourhood, isn't it, and this religion is not appropriate for this place, certainly not for our family and friends. School is surely not the place for allowing the advancement of another religion like this?

Powerlessness: why were we not consulted? What do we know about these people and about whether the children will be properly catered for? Why is it that the only alternative for the children and young people of this area in the evenings and holidays is a religious group such as this?

Some of these questions may be valid; many may not be. However, I suspect that those feelings and questions are played out whenever churches seek to serve young people of other faiths. Underpinning so much of this book is a call for churches to take seriously the command to 'love your neighbour as yourself'. As we engage from a Christian perspective with young people and children, do we offer services reflecting how we, too, would like to be treated? The answer is not to shut up shop and withdraw from an engagement with those of other faiths. Far from it! Nor is the answer to lock up our Christian faith in a tight box, throw away the key as we serve practically and pretend that religion doesn't exist for us. No!

Part of the answer – and it's only part because this is complex and requires a journey unique to people and place – is in standing in *their* shoes. It's back to the listening and learning again. Here are some helpful starting points.

1. *See the young people and children first and foremost as people* – they are not theological problems or trophies. Their world might be

different from ours but they have many of the same likes and dislikes as any other child or teenager. The chances are that they, too, are impossible to get out of bed before 11am on a Saturday morning, have crushes, worry about exam results, get moody, can text for England and wonder, deep down, who they are in this big wide world. And the reality of being a British Muslim, Sikh, Hindu is that a whole mixed bag of cultural and religious influences will be at play in many of those we meet. The second and third generation experience of British identity will belie simplistic judgments such as, 'Well, Hindus always do this don't they?' Well, it probably depends on who you meet!

A musical phenomenon called 'mashing' has grown out of the digital revolution'. It involves mixing music from sometimes quite distinctly different genres and overlaying the beats and instruments of two or more tracks, sometimes fading out elements or emphasising others. Many South Asian background youngsters 'mash' Bollywood music samples with Hip Hop or garage styles, throwing in some R & B along the way. If you glazed over in bemusement at any point in that list, don't worry: suffice it to say they are music styles from the West and East! This mashing is an illustration of what is happening in so much of the cultural lives of British young people of other faiths. Friday may be a day of prayer for some but in the evening, it may be party time in the city bars. A fusion and intermingling which is happening across so many spheres of life requires us to relate to this in order to understand. It is exciting, creative and exhilarating but means that superficial generalisations should be avoided.

2. *They are young people and children who* do *religion* – Tony Blair's former press secretary said that in the Labour Party they 'don't do religion.' World events seem to be changing that statement for the Labour Party, but young people and children of other faiths most certainly 'do religion'. The trouble is, a lot of youth and children's work resources are aimed at communicating Christian truths in a world of people similar to Tony Blair's press secretary. You know the thing: 'recognizing that God-shaped hole', encouraging conversations about faith and spirituality then communicating the idea of a God and what he may be like. It's necessary and good but off-track for a Hindu teenager who prays to a number of idols in his room or a Sikh girl who hears about God regularly at home. Whatever faiths we encounter, for us to connect in conversation

and world view, we must find those areas with which we can agree, and those beliefs with which we differ.

Yes, it's homework time again. What are the core beliefs and practices; what are the texts and places of worship? What is good and 'of God' that I can bless, and where do I see a difference and recognise a distinctiveness in my own Christian faith? The best research is a combination of study, reading, internet browsing and personal asking, visiting, enquiry and listening; because textbooks will only help us part of the way.

3. *Ethical practice is one aspect of tasting the good news* – let's go back to some of the questions and feelings we might have had if another faith group were working among our Christian youth and children. As a parent, I would like my children to be involved in projects and programmes led by people trained and equipped for the task. I would like there to be transparency about the aims and objectives, and to be able to see any of the sessions and meet any of the leaders to talk through what was being provided.

WYSIWYG is a common mnemonic in the obscure world of IT professionals. Pronounce it 'WIZZYWIG'! It stands for 'What You See Is What You Get'. WYSIWYG is a crucial mark of authentic living and something that I believe to be a hallmark of Christian discipleship and mission. Whether our programmes are evangelism-based or community service-based, do people know what they are getting? Have we even bothered to communicate? Who do we go to when we do communicate?

In Birmingham, a holiday club has been run by a group of churches in a Muslim majority area for many years. The club is always oversubscribed and the community welcomes the volunteers with open arms because their children will be served wholeheartedly and with love. Mosque leaders and parents are told the nature of the materials to be used. Bible stories, many of which can also be found in the Qur'an, inform the teaching that accompanies the activities but there is a clear distinction made between the use of the stories as illustrations of what Christians believe and a lesson or moral that can be drawn which is applicable to everyone. The club is therefore very publicly Christian and moral (and this has added potency in many other-faith communities) while enabling the inclusion of all participants, who are free to agree, or not, with the specific calling to follow Christ. It is a wonderful example of a distinctly welcoming Christian service.

It's worth posing some extra questions here. What do the volunteers pray for each morning before the Muslim children arrive at the club? Do they pray for things which in any way contradict the public intentions of the club and all that has been communicated to parents and community leaders? I'm convinced that we can pray that all the children learn more about Jesus, have a great time, establish friendships, feel loved and accepted, grow up with an awareness of God and with tools to follow his ways. But prayers and intentions which undermine the trust established by the club are very questionable. This leads us to the next point:

4. *Choosing another faith in a culture where there is no choice* – for traditional white British cultures, we readily talk about the 'individual' and 'choice'. So much of our language of discipleship is often framed around our 'personal decision' to follow Christ. That is good but it is only one part of the story of commitment. The biblical world view was very different from ours and had a much stronger sense of community decision-making. Community would begin first and foremost with the family, a much larger vision of family than the one we may imagine today, that nuclear family of parents with 2.4 children. Vital to that process of community decision-making is the rite of passage into adulthood and the consequent respect for and deference to elders.

This is something like the world view of many of our other-faith communities. What young Dilip gets up to in the locality would be known and scrutinised not just by his parents but by Auntie Sonia and second cousin Sangeeta down the road. A whole host of near and distant relations will have some authority over the life and direction of the youngster from many other-faith communities. The children and young people simply do not have a choice. This is why Jesus' radical call to discipleship, involving leaving parents, brothers and sisters, was so shocking. Jesus recognised that he had to be the source of primary allegiance. His call took precedence over everything else but that decision could only be decisively made in adulthood, when that freedom, which comes with incredible responsibility, could be exercised. When Paul and Silas were in prison and the earthquake shook the jail, it wasn't just the jailer who would be saved if he believed but his entire family. God was working not with an individual but with a family. Our work needs to be with children and young people but to have a family focus. We need to be looking for what God is doing in families and communities.

So meanwhile, with our children and young people of other faiths, we sow seeds responsibly, faithfully, ethically, fully and publicly Christian but honourably and with grace, encouraging the respect of parents in the communities with which we work.

It's a fine line but as I frequently tell people, 'Doing a club or an assembly once is easy. You can go in, preach hell-fire and damnation and never be invited back. Easy. You can go in and talk of our common humanity, the environment, loving everybody and never ever mention Jesus and with this approach, you will always be invited back. Easy. Doing all these things in such a way that you are faithful to the good news of Jesus, are distinctively Christian, tangibly praying and worshipping people – now that is harder.' I love the idea of Jesus serving, teaching, blessing and healing but always leaving things a little open. Jesus never seemed anxious for a huge following. Rather, with a glance over his shoulder, he'd be sussing out who wanted more, who was really hungry and had been tantalised by the experiences of the kingdom of God among them. You sense that Jesus never compromised on his own identity for an easy life but always seemed to love and serve, generously and transparently.

5. *Dodge the obvious pitfalls* – in practical terms, some aspects of religious observance can, unbeknown to us, be problematic as we serve. It's a very simple issue of respect and understanding. Ignorance can land us in all sorts of trouble and a little more enquiry, research and listening can produce a disproportionate amount of goodwill.

Smeeee: this reminds me of a story from my time in North Africa. I'd been getting to know a local Muslim man called Mounir and I bumped into him in the local market. We shook hands and were chatting away (my side of the conversation a mixture of French and broken Arabic!) when I realized he was still holding my hand. Ten minutes later, in this crowded market, we are still holding hands. Now, I had seen men walking together with hands held and noticed that it was clearly just a local expression of friendship. My mind had clocked this but inside, the stiff upper-lip Englishman was squirming for the moment when he would let go. The thing is, if I had been repulsed by the gesture and moved away from Mounir, I would have insulted him. I would have communicated disrespect. I needed to go through some discomfort in what was natural and customary for me, in order to develop friendship and to allow genuine communication to take place.

In a thousand and one ways, cultural and religious practices may affect the services we provide and the events we organise. In some other-faith cultures, it may be necessary to arrange single-sex events when we are working with young people beyond puberty. We cannot generalise particular faith groups here (remember the 'mashing' that goes on!) but what equivalent youth facilities are there in the area and how do they deal with the gender issue? Have we talked to local community and religious leaders, and what is their approach? As we have noted in earlier chapters, there are times when the church needs to challenge culture as well as affirming it, so you may have to consider whether being sensitive to gender separation is appropriate or an obstacle to your community aims. The point is that the conversation, in prayer and with wisdom, observing and listening, needs to happen.

Food issues are a little simpler and require us to respect the beliefs and practices of others. Thus, many Hindus are vegetarian and most definitely would not eat beef. A trip for Hindu young people to the local carvery would therefore be out of the question! Muslims have to eat *halal* food (meat killed in a certain way) and they would never eat pork. It's worth checking that there is no gelatine in sweets or traces of pork in crisps or other snacks. If in doubt, ask! Many other-faith children are very conscious of the food issues so will err on the side of caution by assuming they cannot eat the food unless told otherwise. Making an effort to find out and cater for those differences will go a long way in us being the distinctly welcoming people we are called to be.

We can easily become paralysed by the possibility of making mistakes. Fortunately, love covers a multitude of cultural gaffs. People know when we are keen to learn and willing to make an effort to be sensitive to the differences. And when we do get it wrong, as we will, it can become an occasion for laughter and intimacy rather than of suspicion and enmity.

A DISTINCTLY WELCOMING APPROACH TO CHRISTIAN PRESENCE IN SCHOOLS

Schools are probably the most common arenas for interfaith mixing. This is where many of the values and perceptions between faiths will be formed and for many churches, an engagement is configured perhaps around a faith school, a faith-based school or in the leading of collective worship and Religious Education lessons.

For schools with a Christian faith foundation, it is important that an explicitly Christian ethos is worked out in the values and practices of that school. Much as we explored the 'distinctive faith' concept for community projects, there is an opportunity to translate clear Christian guidelines in ways which benefit not just Christian young people, but wider society.

One school I know is a jewel of distinctive Christian faith in a multi-faith community. It's a Church of England Voluntary Aided primary school for 3–11 year-olds. It caters for Christian, atheist, Hindu, Sikh and Muslim families. Nearly half of the intake of reception pupils is now Muslim although the ethos is unashamedly based on the Bible and the example of Jesus. The school follows Jesus' teaching that he came so that people might have life in all its fullness (John 10:10). This means not just theological or academic fullness but *all* its fullness. So the school works hard at helping pupils achieve good results and experience the arts, residential activities and sports.

The school follows Jesus' teaching to be servants so constantly looks for ways of improving things for the pupils and the staff. This may be through the teaching or through improving the site, displaying the children's work in creative and imaginative ways or enhancing the lunch menu. Service is after the manner of Jesus who cared for the Samaritans as well as for the Jews. The school doesn't just look out for the Christians but seeks to care genuinely for people of all faiths and none.

The school strives to be a place of forgiveness. This doesn't mean letting pupils (or staff!) get away with wrongdoing with impunity but they are constantly subject to discipline. Bullying is not accepted among pupils or teachers, so both screaming to gain control in the classroom or violence to gain control in the playground are not tolerated. Each day is meant to begin afresh without the holding of grudges, and pupils are helped to understand the consequences of their actions and to take responsibility for them.

This is not meant to be a boast of how much more wonderful and caring this school is than others. Rather, it is meant to show that these good values, to which lots of schools work, are biblical values and can be spoken of in a church school with reference to our text. Being distinctive and welcoming.

Similar principles can operate when teaching about the Christian faith or leading collective worship. First of all, we need to recognise that pupils have to attend school and so are there not by choice but compulsion. It's back to that choice word again. It makes a difference to how we expect the pupils to follow and interact with what is presented. And it is a school, a place of education where we have to work with the school ethos and code and not against it.

One way we can adapt to the fact that attendance is compulsory is to give the pupils a 'mental opt out'. In other words, they might not be able to get up and leave but they can think, 'I don't agree with that' or 'Those beliefs aren't my beliefs or the beliefs of my family'. So, in collective worship, it is important to use sentences such as 'The Bible says that Jesus was God's Son;' or 'Christians believe that Jesus died as a punishment for the wrong things people do;' or 'This festival is important to Christians because it shows how much God loves us as his Creation.' Phrasing truth in this way presents the distinctive whilst acknowledging that these truths are not owned by all and may well not be owned by everyone sharing in the lesson or collective worship. Simply saying, 'Jesus is the Son of God;' or 'we all know why Jesus died, don't we?' rides roughshod over the different faith positions that will be present and is in danger of being an abuse of the privilege that we have within the schools.

Using the Bible is not only central to teaching about our faith but also often interesting to the children, who love hearing the stories, especially those from another faith background. A colleague was explaining the story of Shadrach, Meshach and Abednego and told a school full of Muslim children that Nebuchadnezzar built a statue to show that he was more important than anyone, even God! When this was said, an audible gasp went up and there was a look of genuine shock on the children's faces: how could *anyone* be so godless? As we share the stories, we must aim to illustrate them by reference to our own faith and the Christian tradition but then to explain a moral lesson from the passage so that all can gain something for their own lives.

So with the story of the men who lowered their friend through the roof for Jesus to heal, we might say, 'This teaches Christians that Jesus could forgive sins. This is something only God can do so Jesus must be more than an ordinary man. Christians believe that Jesus is the Son of God. But for all of us, this story challenges us about our commitment to our friends. Would we do that for them? God wants us to care for our friends in the way those men did in the story. Will you care for your friends today?'

The strengths of this approach are that:

- it complies with school regulations, which are a good thing if they protect abuse of cultures and freedoms.
- it allows us to teach deep truths about the Christian faith in an inclusive and respectful way.
- it shows the children that the Bible has something to say to them, even if they are not Christians.
- children learn that the Bible is a book of wisdom which is worth reading, whatever they think about its central message of Jesus

The American church leader and teacher Rob Bell presents a neat picture of two different approaches to sharing what is dear to our hearts. A loving husband might show a photograph of his wife from his wallet: 'Look, she's gorgeous; I love her'. We might be decidedly uncomfortable if he wanted to look at the wallets of other husbands, take out the photographs of their wives and say how ugly they are compared to his! Our task is to so speak of and enact the love of Jesus with and for young people, children and all our communities, without resorting to the slander and abuse of the dearly held beliefs of others.

DISTINCTLY WELCOMING TIPS

- remember that many children and young people do not have the option of being able to exercise a choice of faith. Let us honour families and communities in presenting the Christian story with grace and love, respecting the differences of other faith groups.
- be transparent about the aims of events with children, young people, families and the various communities in which you are working .
- be unafraid of expressing the Christian belief or truth within stories but also bring out principles of behaviour that could be owned by people, whatever their faith. This affirms the Bible and Christian tradition as being useful to all people and worthy of respect even if particular Christian beliefs are not shared.
- where possible, draw on shared beliefs and stories (even if it is as basic as 'We are accountable to God.') to involve and

include people while also highlighting what is distinctive and particular to the Christian faith.
– be committed to a long term engagement which focuses on the family and the community and not simply the individual.

A LA CARTE 🍽 – 2 Kings 5

My name is Naaman. I don't expect that means anything to you but in my country, if you speak my name, people tremble. I'm the captain of the King of Aram's army: Stormin' Naaman they call me. I didn't get where I am today without delivering for my boss. I've an unbeaten stretch that's given our people and my king wealth beyond imaginings. I can fight anyone, command anyone, buy anything, all in the name of my king. There's been this one snag, though: I suffer from leprosy. Yep, one of the supposed untouchables. The disease has left its mark on my appearance, but looks aren't everything. It's the loss of feeling that's the worst of it. The gradual hardening of patches of skin so I can't distinguish hot from cold. You have to harden yourself to have a job like mine. You get used to seeing the face of suffering. Often the best way to get through it is to deaden yourself to all that's around you. So it seems that inside and out, I've a tough skin and you can't get through to me.

The king's been happy to overlook my 'complaint' but it has still caused me to suffer deeply. I kept all this to myself; well that's what I thought. Not for me the intimacy of friendships. I might terrify people. Many say they respect me but they'd never love someone like me. We have this Jewish slave working in my house, helping my wife. She's part of that tribe that worship what they call 'the one true God'. No idols in her room and a distinct way of living that's impressive, even for a slave girl. Rebekah, that's her name; she always works hard and I reckon she's been in the school of hard knocks, too. Maybe we have a lot in common. I don't know what happened to her family or her home. Chances are her family are dead and her home razed to the ground. . . and I would have been ultimately responsible for that. But I've always sensed Rebekah seeing through my hard layers. You know when certain people look at you and you know that they know something more about you? Well, it's like that with Rebekah.

She caught me weeping on the roof recently. My right hand had begun to lose some of its feeling. The leprosy was beginning to take hold and it would be a long slow slide into oblivion. How on earth could you have a commander-in-chief who couldn't wield a sword! She'd found me like that a few times. Rebekah knew I wasn't quite the hard warrior everyone else saw.

Anyway, she tells me about one of their prophets, Elisha. Apparently Elisha is the business. When he speaks, it happens. When he prays, their God answers. Well, they would say that, wouldn't they? They all do – I know because I've tried them. But I'd never tried Yahweh, the 'one God'. And this Elisha, Rebekah says, well, he has a hotline. No incantation necessary. He'll tell you what's what, straight from the horse's mouth.

Now you have to understand, I'm a desperate man. But desperate enough to go to the prophet of a backwater people that we kick around for fun? And it's not like his own people pay him much respect. He's not got any big temple, no wealth or prestige to speak of. We're talking a major step down for Stormin' Naaman to pay a call to this prophet. But I am desperate. I'm gonna cut a long story short because you're guessing that Elisha's God healed me. Well, you'd be right. But I didn't know the half of it when I was heading for that backwater country. Elisha gets me to do something: bathe seven times in their river! Backwater is too grand a word for that muddy puddle he gets me to wade into. I tell him that surely the Tigris and Euphrates would be rivers far more suited for someone of my stature if I have to swim in anything (and they're a lot cleaner, let me tell you!). But no, it's the River Jordan for me. I tell the servants and my lieutenants not to tell a soul. Any stories getting back that General Naaman fancies himself as a hippo and it's the gallows for them!

Well, I was cleaned in that backwater: completely. I remember sitting in the river, waist-deep;, the seventh time. I could feel tingling in my fingers, could see dried skin washing off me, and I giggled like a child. I lay back in the water and just looked at the heavens. Yahweh: that's his name. The One God. There could not be any other who could do this.

I wanted to give this Elisha everything. I told you I'm rich. And this Elisha bloke; well, he looked like he could do with a new suit and a few square meals. But he wasn't having any of it. It was free. Nothing to pay. Gratis. No snags, no penalty clause. He'd had no agenda. Didn't want me to put in a good word for him with the king: nothing. I'd been humbled. This was real love. This was the kind of love and service I'd had glimpses of in Rebekah. This Yahweh was a God worth following.

My mind was racing because it's no easy matter following 'the one God' when you're commander-in-chief of the King of Aram's armies. You see, we have a number of gods and they are our gods for our country, for our land, our sky, our battles. I knew, deep down, there'd be a conflict and this Yahweh wouldn't tolerate a half-hearted following. Yahweh had proved he was God of all. That kind of love demanded you gave everything, because you wanted to.

I tell Elisha my dilemma. The king loves me and he's knocking on a bit; a little doddery on his feet. And I'm the man he chooses to lean on when he enters the temple of Rimmon. I've got to be right by his side when he's bowing to the idol that, I know, is nothing compared to Yahweh. But what do I do now? First of all, the king has given me so much. He's been loyal to me when others would have retired me as soon as the leprosy started. And I love him. He's a good man, a fair king. Secondly, and you gotta understand our world when I say this, I'm dead meat if I refuse. The king is sincere about his faith; really believes it. But he can't have his commander-in-chief refuse him so publicly. There's honour at stake here. Damned if you do, damned if you don't. Choice was something not available to me. I ask if God will forgive me when I bow down in the temple of Rimmon with my master as long as I never offer worship to any other god. Elisha listens. He's a man of few words. And for a prophet, he seems really chilled about the whole deal. He looks at me intently. And he just says, 'Go in peace'. Gulp! What a God! What a people! What a responsibility!

SOUNDTRACK 🎧

Naaman's story prefaces another immersion in the River Jordan. Jesus, King of Kings, identified himself with us in baptism. Humbly sets himself with humanity, in our frailty and weakness. Baptism roots our story in the story of all humans of whatever race and religion. We all fall short. As we choose to die in our sins, God cleanses and forgives us. Take time aside to remind yourself of that potent symbol of our humanity and brokenness. Maybe even wash your hands in a bowl, declaring again God's forgiveness over your life.

Father God, create in me a clean heart
Free of malice and gossip
Free of ulterior motives and secret agendas
Father God, show me your path
Of love and service
Of gift and blessing
For your glory
Amen

TAKEAWAY 🏍

Commit yourself to developing at least one of the three areas covered in this chapter:
1. Encouraging a renewed and informed youth work amongst those of other faiths

2. Having an involvement, whether through RE lessons or collective worship, in a local school with a multi-faith constituency
3. Equipping Christian young people for a multi-faith society. Work with a team within your church to apply some of the principles outlined in this chapter. What would you do differently from before? Outline a plan of action and prayerfully consider a long-term strategy for your church, involving and working amongst young people in a multi-faith context.

BANQUET 🏠
B J Walsh and S C Keesmat *Colossians Remixed* (Paternoster Press, 2005)

HEALTHY APPETISERS 🍎
Tim Sudworth, Graham Cray, Chris Russell *Mission-Shaped Youth: Rethinking Young People and Church* (Church House, 2007)
Gill Marchant and Andrew Smith *Top Tips on Welcoming Children of Other Faiths* (Scripture Union, 2007): practical advice and help for churches wanting to work with children of other faiths, either through church activities or in schools; available by ordering from www.scriptureunion.org.uk
Nigel Pimlott *Faiths and Frontiers: young people in a multi-cultural society* available from Frontier Youth Trust at wwrw.fyt.org.uk

VIRTUAL FOOD 🖱
Richard Sudworth, Andrew Smith and Gill Marchant *Faith Values*: a series of eight Bible studies for church youth groups, a CYFA resource published by CPAS, giving guidelines on understanding and relating as Christians to Islam, Buddhism, Hinduism, Sikhism and New Age spiritualities. Downloadable from http://www.cpas.org.uk/home/bookshop/index.php?site=5
Youth Encounter – http://www.youthencounter.org.uk/ This Scripture Union project supports Christian-Muslim youth dialogue and the site provides excellent guidelines and stories.

Chapter 7

Reconciling with Distinction: Christians as Agents of Unity in a Diverse Society

> *'The problem is not that we don't know each other but that,*
> *too soon, we think we know enough of each other'.*
> Kwame Anthony Appiah

We've managed to get to Chapter 7 without saying much about the 'd' word: dialogue. I hesitate to use this word at all, and avoided using it for the chapter title. It's just so weighed down with images which conjure up something dreary and lukewarm. In popular imagination, there is the idea that 'interfaith dialogue', to give it its proper term, is a forum for middle-aged men – yes, generally men – to discuss the finer points of theology. It's all sage looks and furrowed brows: Christians beating their breasts, saying how exclusivist and imperialistic they are, and other-faith religious leaders agreeing. Days of interfaith dialogue invariably consist of a series of lectures by well-meaning, aged academics with limited connection to the realities of their respective congregations: dialogue as monologues! And statements of intent might be published that focus in on the common grounds of the respective faiths, neatly avoiding conflict, disagreement and grass-roots issues bubbling in the faith communities. That's some people's impression, anyway.

I'm being horribly unfair. Now, more than ever, we need to engage in dialogue with other faiths as a part of our mission of reconciliation and peacemaking. As Chief Rabbi Jonathan Sacks says, 'If religion is not part of a solution, it will certainly be part of the problem.'[1] And the challenge for us is that dialogue,

---

[1] Jonathan Sacks, 'The Dignity of Difference', page 9

whether with a small 'd' or a big 'D' is something in which all of us to engage. This is not an obscure avenue of church life for specialist academic theologians of a certain age and bent. It is the life and breath of witness and neighbourliness that can be practised with conviction, energy and creativity. When Paul describes the gospel as a 'ministry of reconciliation' in 2 Corinthians 5:18,19, I'm encouraged to think that Christians can be genuinely agents of good news: faith does not have to lead to alienation, suspicion and wars. When Jesus pronounces, 'Blessed are the peacemakers', I'm not wondering if he really meant the cheese-makers, but convinced that God is delighted in churches which make it their business to befriend groups with which it might otherwise disagree.

And dialogue need not fit the stereotype I described. Dialogue will sometimes be about finding the common ground, but it will also be about facing up to disagreement and conflict. The bottom line is a commitment to remain friends and good neighbours. It might sometimes be about exploring the niceties of the Islamic doctrine of *tawhid* and the Christian doctrine of the Trinity (don't worry if you got lost in the fog here). But more often it will be about talking over with a Hindu mum at the school gates what you had for Christmas dinner or hearing about the fasting regulations of a Muslim colleague during Ramadan.

So, I aim to redeem the 'd' word for those of us who don't fit the stereotype I described, while also blessing those who do as part of the breadth of what dialogue can be!

Let's step back a bit and try and reflect on where dialogue might fit in the engagement with other faiths. I began the book by drawing some diagrams that represented the common understandings of the relationship between Christianity and other faiths. I suggested that these may hamper the full encounter with other faiths that we see in Scripture. Our primary focus should be reclaiming our identity as Christians, our 'distinctive faith', and that would help in shaping an interaction that could be fully missionary and evangelistic but also humble and welcoming.

It seems that what I am advocating in this book is a plethora of approaches to other faiths: evangelism, community action, dialogue and the rest. And yet these often seem to have competing and contradictory aims. How can this be? Let's try another diagram:

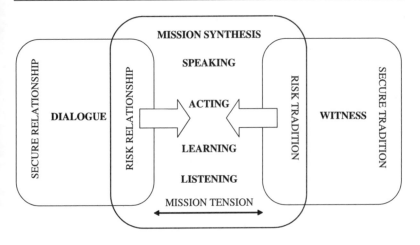

I've attempted to represent what are often seen as the two poles of approach to other faiths: dialogue and witness. In the blue corner is the army of evangelists ready and waiting with their tracts seeing every moment with a person of another faith as an opportunity to talk about Jesus. And in the red corner is a committee of interfaith dialoguers, earnestly determined to affirm that the religions have so much in common. I'm being unfair again, but when I speak in churches, these are the stereotypes I find myself having to overcome. *Now, Richard, you're not one of those dialogue types who thinks we're all going to heaven/you're not one of those arrogant evangelist types who thinks they're all going to hell (delete as appropriate)?* What I attempt to show in the above diagram is that all of us ought to be holding together something of dialogue and witness as we relate to other faiths.

When we focus on dialogue, there is a tendency to a *secure relationship* with the adherent of another faith where commonality and shared humanity are explored. An emphasis on 'witness' would underpin a *secure tradition* where Christian worship, liturgy and the Bible are harnessed to reinforce difference. However, I believe that an authentic encounter with other faiths holds these two poles together; that a truly biblical mission draws from our distinctives *and* calls us into relationship with our fellow humanity.

This is the mission tension which we need to hold together. It is a synthesis, a harnessing of the breadth of God's mission which is the place of Christian service. This creative space, which can hold together dialogue and witness, confirms what has been running through the whole of this book: the gospel both affirms and challenges all cultures and religions. There are features where we discover grace and love. But there are aspects of brokenness and sin. So, if we are *speaking* (witnessing, engaging in dialogue, enjoying a curry, talking over the garden fence) with our other faith neighbours, we need to be able to bring both the 'yes' of Jesus and the 'no' of Jesus. If we are *acting* (campaigning against the persecution of Christians, providing a social action project, working together for the representation of faith groups at national government), we need to be able to bring both the 'yes' of Jesus and the 'no' of Jesus. If we are *learning* (exploring discipleship models for new converts, reading about different festivals and texts, discovering a shared theological idea), again we need to be able to bring both the 'yes' of Jesus and the 'no' of Jesus.

Now clearly there is a spectrum in this mission tension so I'm not necessarily going to be challenging a Hindu acquaintance at the school gates about the treatment of the Christian minority in Nepal. But this goes back to earlier themes about relationships. There is unpredictability and risk. We can't always anticipate what Christ-like challenge or response will be required of us in advance. What is the depth and substance of a relationship when areas of disagreement can never be aired? Conversely, is the God of love honoured by the mockery of a relationship when we never listen, can never receive and never be challenged by the other party? Once again, what allows this mission tension to be authentic is a godly humility and a willingness to open *ourselves* up to the comfort and challenge of Christ.

The 'secure tradition' denies true Christian identity if it never goes out beyond its own boundary to affirm, bless, learn and listen. The distinctive faith we have described exists right in the middle: in that place of risky vulnerability.

Dialogue, then, fits exactly into the mission of the church and is a fitting component of Christian ministry alongside evangelism and community action, and informing both. You see, despite my earlier caricature, I do not believe that evangelism or social action can take place without dialogue with other faiths.

The Roman Catholic Church has described four different categories of interfaith dialogue:

1. dialogue of life – this is the everyday exchange springing from a spirit of openness and neighbourliness.
2. dialogue of action – this involves partnership in issues of shared concern.
3. dialogue of theological exchange – this reflects the specialist theological discussions aimed at deepening mutual understanding between faiths.
4. dialogue of religious experience – this is the sharing of spiritual experiences of prayer and devotions of people of different faiths.[2]

It's helpful to bear in mind these streams of dialogue as we will undoubtedly find ourselves being involved in them all at some point; even if we have not set out to be so. Finding out that a Muslim colleague in the office will not be eating or drinking in daylight hours during Ramadan becomes a relational exchange. It's the stuff of life to find this out. Perhaps you then set out to be sensitive to your colleague by not munching crisps in front of him/her during Ramadan. It's quite possible that you may enter a theological exchange, discussing the nature of fasting. You may begin to share your approach to fasting as a Christian and discover in what ways this is different to Islamic fasting. There might be the simple sharing of the sense of devotion that your colleague feels during Ramadan and in turn your communication of how God speaks to you while fasting as a Christian.

In many and diverse ways, we will be in dialogue with our other-faith neighbours. The watchwords for dialogue are 'openness and neighbourliness'.

This leads me to a crucial discussion in the whole area of dialogue. There are some who would advocate that real dialogue only occurs when you approach the other person willing to have all your convictions and beliefs changed. In a sense, they would say that real openness is only possible when you wipe the slate

---

[2] *Redemption and Dialogue: Reading 'Redemptoris Missio' and 'Dialogue and Proclamation'*, edited by William R. Burrows (Orbis Books 1993), 104

clean, removing all impediments from your faith that may hamper the dialogue. I hope by this stage that you realise that this is *not* the kind of dialogue that fits with a distinctive faith approach. We bring our convictions, our stories, church tradition, truths from the Bible, our prayer-life and the backdrop of the community of worship of which we are a part. These should all inform our dialogue, and if we try to push them away, we are being true neither to ourselves nor to the larger story of God's redemption into which we have joined. The idea that we could ever dissociate ourselves from our convictions and contexts is a nonsense, anyway. Remember the pluralist diagram at the beginning of the book? Well, it's that modernist idea again that we can find a truly objective standpoint from which to judge things that bedevils this kind of dialogue. And it is impossible to achieve. There is no way of standing outside our experiences and beliefs (just ask any good post-modern philosopher!). So the features of distinctive faith at which we have looked are brought to bear in the dialogue of life, action, theological exchange and religious experience.

But the distinctive faith is one of humility, grace and relationship. So, as in any relationship, we bring who we are, but we are not static and unchanging. Most people of faith respect and welcome religious conviction; what they may struggle with is arrogance and an unwillingness to listen and be challenged. I am still humbled by the hospitality and strength of the communities of Sikh and Muslim friends in my neighbourhood. They pose questions to me about the practice of the Christian faith in churches and often drive me to pray and reflect on how we have so much to learn from other faiths. When I visit mosques and see the awe and reverence in the prayer and worship of Muslims, I feel just a little chastened by the way that some of my charismatic worship relegates God to being a chummy agent to supply all my needs.

This type of exchange requires an openness from me to work out the potential of what these relationships and encounters can become in the kingdom of God. As I experience the hospitality or am touched by the reverence, I need to process what I am learning against the Bible, with the community of Christ which is the Church and with the ongoing story of my own prayers and relationship to the Father in the Spirit. We will devote a separate chapter to the issue of spirituality and interfaith mission but suffice to say that a distinctive faith enables dialogue to be both authentic and formative in our Christian discipleship as we remain rooted in our Christian disciplines.

Andrew Smith of Scripture Union, in his running of youth dialogue events, has compiled some guidelines which I believe are immensely helpful for all of us:

- we will listen to what everyone has to say
- we will be honest in what we say
- we will respect each other's views, even if we disagree with them
- we will not tell other people what they believe, but allow them to tell us
- we will acknowledge both similarities and differences between our faiths
- we will not judge people here by what some people of their faith do
- we will not try to force people to agree with our views
- we can ask for a discussion to be stopped if we feel uncomfortable with what is being said
- we will make an effort to get along with everyone, regardless of their faith, gender, race or age

What these guidelines do is allow each party to be true to itself. As we have reflected on the distinctive faith concept, in dialogue and in any constructive relationship, we are also giving space for the other party to be true to itself. This is a faith of the public square because it's in the genuineness of an interaction that our faith is road-tested. *Why do you believe that? What do Christians do in church? How does it help you? Are you just interested in trying to change me or do you really respect me?* It is good for us to reflect on all these questions and more. They throw us back on to our traditions, the Bible and the church. And as we treat these questions seriously, we can deepen our relationship with God and connect back to others with maturity, communicating our faith to them in ways that make sense in their world.

Some of the above guidelines are especially relevant in a world of religious conflict. The determination to respect other's views, even if we disagree with them, is crucial to distinctive faith in a multi-faith world. We might verbally agree that faith is a matter of choice and cannot be forced on anyone but do we sincerely release people to make their own choices? Again, truthful relationships require us to avoid making communication conditional on agreement. There are similarities to affirm and differences to acknowledge. And relationships are encounters which refuse to be pre-cast and determined by other people. I don't know whether you've ever had the experience of someone trying to match-make for you. Matchmaking can work wonderfully, but often the parties themselves are left feeling quite powerless. There can be the feeling of being forced into a relationship created by someone else's vision of each individual: a vision which doesn't match up with the experiences of the pair involved. We need to find out for ourselves the nature of the other party: hopes and fears, dreams, joys and disappointments. Isn't this what we would expect for ourselves? I do not want to be pre-judged by the behaviour of some Christians in the world or by the media view of the church as a muddled, irrelevant club. So let us approach people of other faiths as individuals, being open to their unique story.

The intention of this book has been to provide a general resource for Christians working with a whole range of different faith groups. At this point, I'll depart from the script and address the specific issue of dialogue with Muslims. We need no reminding of the terrors which have been associated with 'Islam' and 'Muslim', just as we ought to be conscious of the horrors which have been associated with 'Church' and 'Christian'. In this day and age, we need to make a special effort to relate, befriend and talk to Muslims without pre-judging their goodwill and their theology. There, I said it! Surely that is what we would want for ourselves? Let us love our neighbours likewise and not impose *our* view of 'what *they* think', 'what *they* do' without having heard and experienced these things at first-hand from this *particular person*.

The guidelines have been developed particularly in a context of dialogue for young people with especial concern that they are given appropriate protection from any abusive action and that families can be confident in the reasonable quality of any discussion. Therefore, the possibility of closing down any avenue of inquiry if a party feels uncomfortable is a helpful get-out clause. Even as adults, there will be times when we feel pressurised and intimidated in dialogue. We may be feeling particularly threatened by a line of questioning or ill-prepared to respond to some probing theological accusation. A truthful dialogue, like a truthful relationship, will be clear about boundaries. There may well be times when we need to say, 'Stop!' There will be occasions when what started out as an equal exchange with a particular agenda suddenly turns into a very unequal exchange with a very different and imposing agenda which makes a person feel cheated and vulnerable. It is right and proper that we can step back when appropriate.

However, here's the twist in the tail! Appropriate dialogue also means that we respect other people's willingness to draw boundaries when *they* feel threatened and uncomfortable or where the agenda has changed. In wanting to be slightly irreverent about the traditional world of interfaith dialogue, I'm attempting to remove from it connotations of mystery and intellectualism. What we are talking of here is little more than the nitty-gritty business of relationship-building informed by a clear sense of who we are in Christ.

I've heard and read of Christians saying that dialogue is just a 'slippery-slope'. You start doing that and then you lose all focus, all radical evangelistic zeal. I actually think that the slippery slopes are on either side of the diagram I presented. If all we do is talk to each other *within* our faith and talk *at them* outside of our faith, we're on a slippery slope to missing God's mission beyond the church in the world and becoming indulgent and self-satisfied. If l we are simply *talked at* from those outside our faith, forgetting how we *talk with* each other within our faith, we're on a slippery slope to failing God's missionary call and becoming bland and impotent.

There's a buzzword going around the interfaith studies world – *reciprocity*. That's yet another word, appropriated for dialogue and mission, which makes a lot of sense in relationships in general. Reciprocity is a good goal in any relationship and especially so with other faiths. It assumes differences between parties because there is evidently an enriching transfer from one to another. And it presupposes a relationship of equality. There, that word again! Diversity *and* equality. But here's the snag. So many of our relationships with people of other faiths are not reciprocal. I know of a number of church leaders who would like to establish regular meetings with other faith leaders but those others are not in the least bit interested. I also know Christian students of other religions who would dearly love to see some of their other-faith counterparts show even embers of curiosity into Christian theology. Here in Britain, there are endless discussions about the liberty of religious minorities and the freedom to practice difference and how our society may be helpfully nurturing choices of faith. Yet we have countless examples of those same minority faiths, in a position of majority around the world, exacting religious oppression on Christians and other dissenting groups. I'm conscious even as I write this that I'm pressing on a raw wound in the Church and within many other faith groups today. How on earth can reciprocity work in these cases?

I think I can only answer for the Christians. I'm going to throw out that old chestnut of the distinctive faith concept again. We looked at core Christian beliefs such as incarnation, grace, the Trinity, redemption and resurrection. Our *goal* is reciprocity, but *even if we do not receive anything in return*, our path is one of selfless love. That was a bit preachy, I'm afraid, so I'll try to put it another way. If we follow a relational God, who gives of himself, even to the extent of dying, if we follow a God who loves us freely and whose offer of life does not require that we be perfect or even better, if the God we worship reaches out, speaks and crosses boundaries. . . then maybe we should, too!

And it is hard. So setting up dialogue events, asking about the practice of other religions, researching and listening, and sometimes having no evidence of a similar interest is dispiriting. Helping religious minorities to be viewed in a more positive light in Britain, assisting them to engage fully and in an informed way with local and national government, and doing this when Christians are being persecuted in countries by other-faith majorities, can be deeply depressing. But the way of the cross is also the way of resurrection and hope!

These struggles need to be part of the dialogue process, too, and the best examples of this sort of dialogue do not shirk the conflicts, fears and inequalities as long as they are communicated with respect and grace, in authentic relationship. As is so often the case in God's economy, this path of selfless love is also laden with the surprise and blessing of God's transformation, a transformation which may well come in the guise of a partner from another faith.

The more I read, the more that I wonder if we should be joining forces with people of faith. Maybe the real opposition are secularists in our country?

There is clearly a lot more we can have in common with those of other faith than we may imagine. In a world struggling for religious literacy, Christians are at least able to empathise with the motivations and total demands of a life that is more than just the here and now. There are very many moral issues in other-faith communities that Christians can identify with that the wider secular society find mysterious or irrelevant. There are some who would view dialogue with other faiths as a vehicle for a wider "faith coalition" that exerts power to put God on the national agenda. It's even been put to me that Muslims, Sikhs and Hindus could be "co-belligerents" against a secularising agenda in Britain. Leaving aside my allergy to the idea of Christians ever being belligerents (soldiers) against other groups, this thinking is in danger of slipping out of the distinctly Christian welcoming model I would advocate.

All people are made in the image of God and yet are broken and in need of God's grace and wholeness. *Even* fundamentalist secularists, rationalist humanists and politically correct local councils! As Christians, we will find blessing and rejection, encouragement and discouragement across all faiths and none. Our task is to love and serve, seeking out in hopeful and vulnerable expectation those individuals we can work with, those that share similar values, not pre-judging nor predicting. Being distinctly welcoming will always mean there will be and ought to be a level of abrasion with other groups. There might be agreed goals, but there will doubtless differences in how we get there. More risky vulnerability I'm afraid to say!

Here are some summary challenges on interfaith dialogue to get you started:

- if your church community has a place of worship of another faith nearby, make it your business to ensure that the church

leadership has regular neighbourly connections with that group. The 'dialogue' can be as simple as discussing the local environment and mutual welfare of spiritual leaders, to programmed theological discussions and collaboration in local politics
- if you live near people of another faith or work closely with one of them, ask about their faith. Show an open interest; this will usually be honouring to them and not insulting. Is there a way of naturally creating intentional opportunities to learn more about each other's faith?
- you have seen the guidelines for dialogue, primarily produced for youth groups. Why not try putting these into practice for a Christian youth group you know or for an adult house or cell group? Make sure you have fun if you take this on! Dialogue is not all about serious conversations!

DISTINCTLY WELCOMING TIPS:

- be yourself!
- be honest.
- listen and enquire: be prepared to grow in your faith in Jesus as you face questions arising from the challenge of hearing about someone else's faith.
- don't compare the best of your own faith with the worst of another's faith: remember the doctrine of original sin! In practice, that means we should be unafraid of owning up to Christian failure and therefore the forgiveness and hope of the cross.
- when you are uncomfortable during dialogue with someone from another faith, do not be afraid of seeking out other Christians, to pray, read the Bible and to worship, and re-centre yourself in the Christian story.

A LA CARTE 🍽 – 1 Corinthians 13
If I can preach so that a congregation touches heaven and 50 minutes feels like five but have not love for people of other faiths, I am only a scratching nail down a blackboard or a car alarm on a peaceful night. If I speak truth courageously and fearlessly, am skilled in counselling and the fine arts of spiritual direction, and if my prayers heal cancers, but I have not

love for Hindus, I am nothing. If I devote all my free time to the homeless and choose to live on a sink-estate as an incarnational witness but have not love for Sikhs, what's the point?

Love is patient with Muslims, love is kind to Jews. It does not envy secularists, it does not boast, it is not proud. It is not rude to Jains, it is not self-seeking, it is not easily angered by Buddhists, it keeps no record of wrongs by atheists. Love does not delight in evil but rejoices with the truth. It always protects the weak and vulnerable of other faiths, always trusts, always hopes, always perseveres in the midst of a multi-faith society.

Love never fails the local imam, the Buddhist priest, the guru and the rabbi. But where there are prophecies, they will cease; where there are tongues, they will be stilled; where there is knowledge, it will pass away. For our grasp of what God is doing in the midst of all this diversity is only partial and we prophesy in part, but when perfection comes, the imperfect disappears. When I was a child, I talked like a child, I thought like a child, I reasoned like a child. When I became a man, I put childish ways behind me. Now we see but a poor reflection as in a mirror; then we shall see face to face. Now I know in part; then I shall know fully, even as I am fully known.

And now these three remain: faith, hope and love. But the greatest of these is love.

SOUNDTRACK 🎧
These three remain: faith, hope and love.
And the greatest? Love.
The hardest, the costliest
But the best.
Just like the Beatles sang,
'All you need is love'.
And God is love.

Father God, we need you,
The world needs you,
The church needs you,
I need you.

Give me faith to hear you,
Hope to see you,
Love to be like you.

In being a friend to others
May I become more like you.
Amen.

TAKEAWAY

Look at the diagram of dialogue and witness. Can you trace your own journey of faith in that diagram? Is there a sense in which you have moved in your own understanding of your approach to other faiths, even as you have read this book? Why not list some of those things which have brought you closer to God through a relationship with someone of another faith. Now write down some of those things you have found out about a person of another faith with which you have struggled and which go against your own understanding of God. Look at the two lists. Thank God for his love and grace in Jesus; ask God to keep you faithful and humble and that he might show you areas of encouragement and bless-ing but also those areas that need to come under his searchlight and transformation.

BANQUET

G D'Costa *The Meeting of Religions and the Trinity* (T & T Clark, 2000)

HEALTHY APPETISERS

B D McLaren *A Generous Orthodoxy* (Youth Specialties, 2004)
C Moucarry *Faith to Faith: A Christian Arab Perspective on Islam and Christianity* (IVP, 2001)

VIRTUAL FOOD

The Interfaith Network – www.interfaith.org.uk – works to encour-age communication between faiths.
The Church of England's *'Presence and Engagement'* report on churches in a multifaith context is available to download from www.cofe.anglican.org/info/interfaith/presence.pdf It provides an overview of the church's challenge to mission and dialogue with helpful statistics and stories.
The Christian-Muslim Forum – http://www.christianmuslimforum.org/ resourcing a national strategy for Christian-Muslim dialogue.
Peacemakers site – http://www.peacemakers.tv/how.html – a hub for excellent multimedia resources helping to encourage under-standing of other faiths with an appreciation of the differences as well as similarities.

Youth Encounter – http://www.youthencounter.org.uk/ – this Scripture Union project supports Christian-Muslim youth dialogue and the site provides excellent guidelines and stories.

Chapter 8

Bringing it all Back Home: a Church that Welcomes and Includes

'The gospel is about grounding heaven'.   Bishop James Jones

Churches can be the most uncomfortable places! I'm not talking now about the sort of discomfort you get from prophetic preaching or a serene moment of worship when you come face to face with the grandeur of God. No, I'm talking about the general ambience. I don't think I'd ever realised how uncomfortable churches could be until I had children. A simple attendance in your local worshipping community is suddenly charged with the adrenaline and stress of, 'Will the preacher drag on and break into my toddler's sleep time, turning him into Hannibal Lecter for the rest of the day?' Or, 'Does the church think we're awful parents because my daughter screamed out, 'I hate you, daddy!' in the middle of a ten-minute quiet Celtic reflection?' At one church I know, the pews have doors on the end of each row – and let's face it, the 'pews' bit is bad enough for children. The first time I was there and noticed the doors, my heart sank. What does every child under ten want to do to a small wooden door with a big brass ring on it? Keep banging it very loudly!

The thing is, we're learning ever so slowly to accommodate the practical differences and needs of various members of churches. So, rightly, wheelchair ramps are built, hearing aid loops set up in the PA and children and babies catered for because we want everyone to participate and connect with the life of the church. Their respective ages and abilities mean we all need to change because our differences are not indicative of what 'being a Christian' is all about. But this is where I want to make my point. We too often forget the cultural attributes that people bring with them and fail to adapt ourselves to the diverse histories brought into church.

These cultural attributes people bring make church an exceedingly uncomfortable place because the majority culture is often not aware of the barriers and struggles presented. This is most keenly felt when we consider people with another faith background as they journey towards Christ or make efforts to integrate into a local church.

Let me introduce you to Kumar. Kumar is a Baptist minister in London and I'm going to let him tell his story:

'I came to the UK as a child and have been brought up as a Hindu, in the Brahmin caste. As a teenager and Hindu, I underwent the "thread ceremony", a kind of rite of passage for a Brahmin Hindu, and this sowed the seeds for my spiritual search out of Hinduism. You see, as a Brahmin, I am from a superior caste, and in the ceremony I was elevated into a status with which I felt very uncomfortable. There were old men and women bowing at my feet, treating me with incredible deference. And I struggled with that. I knew deep down I was just a young guy and that this kind of divisiveness in religion was ridiculous and offensive.

'On going up to university, I studied chemistry and this just raised more questions for me about my Hindu faith, while I was still able to accept that God did exist. And this is where I first met evangelical Christians. Apart from hearing that my grandma was going to hell, I heard the claims of Jesus Christ as unique Saviour. I couldn't return to a faith riddled with division and began to talk with Christians and read the Bible. I was a bit of a problem at Bible studies because I asked all sorts of awkward questions but in May 1985, I understood the heart of the Christian message in terms of Christ's death for my sins, and accepted his offer of forgiveness and salvation.

'As I have walked on this journey of faith, I have begun to have some nagging questions about the model of Christianity which I joined. I realise as I look back that Christians have a sense of cultural and moral superiority over those of other faith traditions. Because Christians believe that they worship the one true God, then how they live, their culture, traditions and practice, must of course be the best and most authentic way to live. Now when I use the term "Christian", I mean the dominant Christian presence for the past 500 years, which has, of course, been Western European Christianity.

'This sense of superiority has permeated the Christian community for a long time and it is deeply embedded within the mindset. When I crossed the religious boundary, I discovered that issues relating to my culture, identity, allegiance, sense of belonging and acceptance had also been deeply disturbed. This disturbance should be universal for all humanity, but in Britain today, as when I became a Christian 21 years ago, the disturbance is greater for those who come to faith from different religious convictions.

'When I first became a Christian, I could see nothing in Hinduism that was good. Hinduism had nothing to teach me about God. I understand my faith in a very personal manner; it is a living, daily relationship with God, and an uncomfortable shift has been taking place. I have begun to think that other faiths and cultures can contribute to my understanding of God. And this is threatening. To countenance such thoughts seemed, initially, like a betrayal of God or that I was being disloyal. I was also fearful that by acknowledging that there was anything positive in Hinduism, I was giving ground to the opposition and undermining my ability to share the good news with them. It has been a huge emotional challenge.

'There has also been an intellectual challenge. I know more about Hinduism as a Christian than I ever did as a Hindu. In my early years, I read many books about Hinduism, but my narrow Christian mindset led me to read them in either a defensive or offensive manner. I felt I had to defend my new faith by dismissing anything positive that I encountered within Hinduism, sometimes labelling it as "of the devil". To advance my own faith, it was as if I needed to denigrate Hinduism and find negatives there to attack. Needless to say, this approach was less than helpful when trying to communicate with my family!

'There has been a cultural challenge, too. I felt that I was pulled in different directions and didn't know quite where I fitted. Hindu? Indian? British? Christian? None of these labels sat easily on me.

'Events in my life began to undermine the entrenched position from which I started out at. In October 1985, five months after I'd become a Christian, an acquaintance at university died in his sleep. I went to see a Christian who told me, as if she were telling me it was raining, "Phil's in hell". Two years later, a close and very supportive family friend suddenly died. He was a

117

devout non-Brahmin Hindu. I'm yet to meet a Christian who displays the fruits of the Spirit in the way that this man did. I knew that my friends would tell me that he was burning in hell. So I didn't say anything to them about him!

'His death started me on a journey to discover more about Hinduism and also what I believed and why I believed it. From 1988 to 1993, I lived as a Christian in a Hindu household. It was a time when I had to face up to my parents' spiritual journey as Hindus and I had to interact with the spiritual journeys of other committed Hindus. All of us need an encounter with a person of another faith who challenges our preconceived ideas; someone who forces us to think outside the box. My brother was one such person. He asked some very tough questions. Why wouldn't I attend the religious functions for the family at the temple and accept offerings made in the temple? I used to refuse to do both. I feared that I would give the wrong impression to my parents and that I was being disloyal to my faith.

'My brother pointed out the following facts to me:

1. However much my parents struggled to accept my Christian faith, they'd always love me and want the best for me.
2. "Though you may not agree with the external form of what they do, can you see that at the heart of what they do there is love and care for you?"
3. "When you refuse their requests, you may think that you are standing up for your faith, but in reality you are missing the point because they are showing love in the only way they know and you're trampling on that love".

'This encounter and exchange, sometimes quite heated, which continues to this day, enabled me to return to Scripture with fresh eyes and to discover some obvious truths which are so easily overlooked. These are some of my theological reflections which are continually evolving. They are not set in stone but are still quite fluid and able to be remoulded:

Humanity is Created in his Image (Genesis 1:27) – so non-Christians bear the image of God. Therefore there is in each and every person something that I can learn from

Creation Bears Witness to God the Creator (Romans 1:20) – those of other faiths who seek to follow a Creator rather than the created may receive some revelation that can teach me something about who God is.

We Serve a Missionary God – God is more interested in the welfare of human beings than we are. It would be entirely within the character of a God of love and grace to be already reaching out and making himself known to people of other faiths

Reinterpret Christ's Uniqueness through the Cross – the human condition is characterised by a loss of innocence before God in the Garden. Jesus' death on the cross, bestowing the gift of forgiveness, restores our lost freedom before God. Therefore, I should approach other faiths with humility, knowing that all I enjoy is a gift, not earned.

'Taken together, these reflections allow me to be true to my Christian faith and the good news that has been embodied in my own life. But as I relate to my family and others of different faiths, I need to come with humility. I do not know everything. There is good which I can learn, and God can teach me through the person of another faith.

'In my work for London Baptist Churches, I am given the task of encouraging churches of diversity and racial inclusion. As they engage with other faith communities and help individuals on a journey towards Christ and discipling new converts, I recognise many of the pitfalls and challenges I experienced and encountered. Here are the two main ones for me:

The Pastoral Challenge – people often have no idea of the pastoral consequences of a Hindu, Sikh, Muslim or Jain becoming a Christian. For my family, it was like setting off a huge bomb in the house. It affected their lives at many different levels:

- in terms of their faith, my mother said that the family was being punished because my father had failed to perform certain prayers for his dead parents. The shifting of the blame on to him didn't go down too well, as you can imagine!
- I refused to attend the temple with them, and this prompted questions from their friends about my absence. They were too embarrassed to tell them that I'd become a Christian.
- they also felt that my faith undermined their standing in their local community as good Brahmin caste Hindus. They feared that it would have a detrimental affect on my sister's marriage prospects.

- as first generation immigrants, their faith and culture had given them a sense of cohesion, unity and purpose, and I had sabotaged all that.
- they were also concerned for my welfare because they were aware of Christian cults.

'There was plenty of emotional blackmail, as I was repeatedly told that I would drive them to a premature death. I was in need of pastoral support from people who would understand. My parents were also in need of pastoral support, though it would have been impossible for them to receive it, as they were ashamed of telling their Hindu priest about my conversion. Suggesting my pastor could offer to pray for them would have been adding fuel to the fire!

The Galatian error and its consequences – the Judaisers in Galatia wanted the Gentile Christians to become Jews and follow Jewish customs in order to follow Christ. The confusion of gospel and culture which forces new believers to adopt the customs and practices of those sharing the faith has led to disastrous results all over the world. I remember being at a presentation in London when a group of new Hindu converts to Christianity shared their testimonies. They proceeded to rubbish their traditional dress as pre-Christian and pre-modern and spoke in glowing terms about how as Christians, they now wore jeans and T-shirts. The largely white gathering cheered and applauded, unwittingly reinforcing the strangest ideas of what it means to be Christian.

'For many of those of other faiths, the impression they receive is that being an authentic Christian means being truly British. Even if we might have baulked at the attitudes to Indian culture of the London presentation, implicit in church life is the superiority of British culture. At the church I attended as a student, I never once heard a positive comment about my Indian culture. In fact it would be true to say that I have never heard anything about Indian culture in any church, in any sermon or other forms of teaching. What I actually heard was overwhelmingly negative: talk of idolatry and the need to save souls. The direction of my discipleship seemed to be about encouraging practice of my faith in a manner that bore no resemblance to my cultural heritage. It seemed that I had to abandon my cultural ties and to embrace Western or European practices, because this is 'real' Christianity.

'So why do I and so many others go along with this situation? Put simply, I had no models or examples to follow and I was being told that this is the best way to practise my faith. I had an identity crisis. My brother used to call me a "coconut". Do you know what that means? Brown on the outside but white on the inside. By embracing Christianity, I had embraced the white man's religion and so abandoned my Asian culture and values. In light of the recent colonial past, my conversion was a real slap in the face for my parents. From my family's perspective, I had abandoned everything that was precious and important to them and embraced foreign values.

'I had a desire to defend my Indian heritage but also had the struggle of not wanting to compromise my faith. Baptism was a huge milestone for me and a point of great conflict with my father. He said that by being baptised I was rejecting my birthright to take his funeral; the emotional screws were really turned. Out of guilt, I responded that perhaps I could take part if it meant so much to him: 'Huh! You're a fickle and unprincipled man who can't stand by his faith!' he replied.

'Could I be a Christian and an Indian at the same time? Did I have to be a brown sahib to be a Christian? My family were calling me a coconut and I was saying, 'I'm not a coconut'. At church, though, in a hundred and one ways, I was being told, 'You must become a coconut'. I had become a foreigner to my own people. I couldn't even enjoy South Indian classical music. Yehudi Menuhin appreciated it and applauded it but my Christian friends called it "squeaky bongo music."

'A stranger to my own culture and community, how could I even convey the good news of Christ to them? There were no bridges of understanding and commonality; my Hindu friends became increasingly alienated from me.'

Kumar is not alone in having had these experiences. Whether converts are Hindu, Sikh, Muslim, Jain, or Buddhist, churches can be especially uncomfortable places for followers of Christ from different religious backgrounds. It's important that we gain a sense of the big picture before making suggestions which can release people like Kumar to be the Christians God has called them to be within their own culture.

We get a glimpse of the big picture in the Revelation of John. Put aside all those odd ideas you may have that Revelation is a book giving us a code to decipher Middle Eastern politics, the European Union and whether credit cards are a tool of the anti-Christ! Basically, we have a story in picture form of where the church is heading. So, this vision of the new city, Jerusalem, 'made of jasper, gold and pure as glass' symbolises so much of where the main trajectory of the Bible's story line is heading. Jerusalem, that seat of Yahweh, place of promise and covenant, is broadened out into this huge expanse that is clear and spotless, magnificent and transparent. God is at the centre of this, the city as symbol of the created world renewed and restored. And what of the church? There isn't one. No temple, no synagogue, no 'holy space'. Because everything is holy, just as all suffering is gone and all tears have been shed.

There is no demarcation between the sacred and the secular, because God fills all with his Spirit of newness and holiness. And God's people are there worshipping! It's a glorious picture. And what do you notice about God's people? They come from every tribe and tongue, language, people and nation. How could you know that, you should ask? Because they look different and sound different; their worship comes from the heart of each tribe and tongue.

This is no cosy vision of *everyone* enjoying the new creation and all roads leading to the new city. It's quite clear that John's Revelation is crunch time for judgement: for a division of the faithful and the unfaithful, day and night. But the new creation is one of immense diversity and creativity! We should expect it to be like this, as we worship and follow a relational, creative God. The vision is not a bland soup of cultures which can conveniently be pictured as blonde, blue-eyed Swedes singing hymns, surrounded by chubby babies with wings. This is the rich diversity of God's world fulfilled in the life of Christ, who is the focus of adoration.

Kumar's journey towards Christ was prompted by a reaction against what he saw as the divisiveness of the Hindu religion. Sadly, if we collude with a model of Christianity which is white and British, we fall into a trap similar to the one Kumar had originally reacted against in Hinduism. Steve Chalke, the founder of 'Faithworks', talks of it as the difference between a purée and a fruit salad! God wants a fruit salad of flavours where we can see the likeness of Christ in the cultural stories of South India, Pakistan, second generation British immigrants, inner-city skaters, suburban professionals. We are to bring our gifts from all these cultures and more to each other, before Christ. You see, the vision of Revelation is not just a comforting snapshot of the hereafter but a goal towards which we work as we bring forgiveness, healing, justice and righteousness from the throne of Jesus.

Kumar has developed some guidelines for a better understanding by British churches of the journeys of other-faith communities towards Christ, exploring how we can be agents of the good news that affirms the fullness of Jesus in every culture. Here are some initial reflections on how *our* culture can either help or hinder the process of engaging in cross-cultural mission, remembering that our culture is similarly a mix of good and bad and that Christ through his incarnation redeems *all* cultures to himself:

1. *Lose the British reserve!* The British reserve comes across as being rude and standoffish. People the world over love to talk, but Hindus, Muslims, Sikhs and others who feel that their culture and traditions have been overlooked love to talk even more. So genuinely engage in conversation.

2. *Embrace their cultural practices.* In this way you affirm another person's culture and tradition. This is particularly important for older generation Hindus, Muslims and Sikhs living in the UK. Food, clothing, sitting on the floor, eating with your fingers, taking your shoes off when you enter their house. In these ways, you become a Hindu to the Hindu and a Muslim to the Muslims.

3. *Don't be over-sensitive.* Fear of causing offence can often be a stumbling block to constructive engagement. Hindus, Muslims, Sikhs, Buddhists and Jews will not expect you to know and understand their beliefs, practices and cultures, so simply ask what is appropriate and inappropriate.

4. *Don't be afraid of speaking about your faith.* Other faiths are inextricably intertwined with their culture. There is no secular/sacred divide, so, without preaching, just be open about your faith. Don't feel shy telling them that you pray. Be natural about your faith, and that will dismantle many of their preconceived ideas about Christians.

5. *Understand people's complaints, misunderstandings and fears.* Take time to listen to the criticisms of other groups, their anger and their misunderstanding of the church, without being hurt and becoming defensive.

6. *Permit difficult questions.* Western rational culture with its objectivity and certainty is a legacy we hold on to in the church but it is of mixed value. Many Asian spiritualities are comfortable with mystery, and it is important that we demonstrate our humility by qualifying our propensity to strident judgments. We do not know everything, and we, too, are part of a culture which is both affirmed and judged.

Now I'm beginning to feel uncomfortable! This all seems like it's one-way; like we have to do all the changing.

We do have to make a lot of changes, it's true. But I'd say three things to that. First of all, they will always have a lot more changing to do. Secondly, this is the tiniest part of what God has done in incarnating Himself into human culture. When we do this, we are joining in God's work and God's ways. Thirdly, we receive so much when we do this. The joys and discoveries of God's abundance in the richness of this diverse world are wonderful when we encounter them. Sure, it makes for some tough decisions in church life but I see it differently. It's not a question of whether we can risk uncomfortable change in church but can we risk missing out on all we would receive as we learn, pray and worship with brothers and sisters from different backgrounds and cultures?

I have a friend from a Sikh background who reminds me that as Christians, we are very good at challenging people from other faiths to make a decision for Christ: to leave all and follow him. As my friend Pall says, those from other faiths often genuinely leave all behind them: families, friends and culture. What they often receive in return is a Sunday morning meeting! It's a poor trade-off because many of our other-faith neighbours come from deeply interwoven and supporting communities. The hour or so we give to weekly worship and prayer, and the nodding, 'Fine' to the cursory, 'How are you?' over cheap coffee and rich tea biscuits can be an insulting parody of the kingdom community to which Christ calls us.

Here are some tips from Kumar to help churches become more attractive places to people from different faiths, especially Asian spiritualities:

i. **A warm, welcoming and loving community** – community is critical for Asians, Africans, Latin Americans and Caribbeans and a warm and effusive welcome is essential. You may say, 'That's not me' or 'That's not my culture'; well, you'll need to make changes just as they'll need to make changes.

ii. **Worship and teaching which seeks to be inclusive** – you could fuse Eastern and Western styles. Use sitar recordings and symbolic responses as acts of worship. Sikhs and Hindus are used to tasting food and drink as an act of worship. So incorporate different senses in Christ-centred worship. Bring some colour, if necessary, into the church building or place of worship, draping sari materials, lighting candles. Some people from a Muslim background may be very uncomfortable with singing so experiment with readings, reflections, listening to devotional music.

iii. **Visible presence of ethnic minorities in the life of the Church** – if those 'at the front', taking collections, playing music, teaching in Sunday School do not represent different ethnicities, then those who come will conclude that they don't have a part in the life of the church.

iv. **Representative leadership** – this is critical because only by having leaders from different perspectives will you hear different opinions and views then act appropriately. If you are forever second-guessing, you will get it wrong.

v. **Genuine pastoral care** – both for the new believer and somehow for their family. This needs to be ongoing. You need to be aware of what is happening at the individual, family and community level

vi. **Flexibility about church commitment** – family pressure may make church attendance hard. Some will not tell their family about their new faith or will have to balance wider family commitments around celebrations which may conflict with church events to retain a sense of their roots and respect of their culture.

vii. **Understand their background or at least be willing to learn** – making an effort to know their story helps them to be made to feel welcome.

viii. **Positive pictorial representations** – don't reinforce media stereotypes. Are our church images of African and Asian people always associated with poverty and abuse? This sends out a message of the superiority of the West. Present pictures of Asian and African joy and creativity.

ix. **Intercessory prayer** – cover the globe! Don't just pray for Britain but be concerned about developments across the world

x. **Induction into church life** – help newcomers to understand what is happening in the service. Why do you stand, sit, sing? What happens next, who does what? All these things will be alien to someone of another faith

xi. **Don't make them into a trophy** – they are human beings not scalps to be paraded

I love it in the letter to the Ephesians (3:1-7) when Paul talks of the fact that Jews and non-Jews have access to God's inheritance through Jesus. In verse 7, the simple reconciliation that occurs between the Jewish and Gentile cultures as they worship Christ is 'the gospel'. There is something of the essence of the good news when people from different cultures worship Christ together. When former Sikhs, Hindus, Muslims and Buddhists come together with white Britons in their worship of Jesus, the gospel is being made known and embodied. I pray that our churches may become places of welcome and diversity in Jesus' name.

A LA CARTE 🍴 – Acts 15:1-35
The Council at Jerusalem – Minutes of the Meeting of AD 35

Attendance:	*Paul, Barnabas, Peter, James, Judas, Silas, Mark, five Pharisees (anonymous) following the Way of Christ and all the apostles and elders of the church in Jerusalem*
Chair:	*Peter*
Apologies:	*none (though the secretary would like to apologise for the repeated omission of the names of female elders and apostles; this is hoped to be rectified when Paul's letters are edited for churches in the region.)*
Minutes of Previous Meeting:	*approved (please note the correction of 'Saul' to 'Paul')*

Matters Arising: *'Policy for integration of non-Jews into the Church' – single urgent Agenda item*

The matter under consideration was whether Gentiles should be circumcised, like Jews, after demonstrating their commitment to Christ and prior to initiation into the church. Peter advocated that expecting an extra load to be laid on them would be unreasonable. God clearly had been working among them without the extra baggage of having to become Jewish (extra baggage that was heavy enough for a true Jew to bear anyway!). No outward sign was necessary to gain acceptance by Christ.

Barnabas and Paul supported Peter's argument with a spirited recounting of all that God was doing with the Gentiles who were coming to Christ. In fact, much of the meeting became sidetracked in worship as Paul and Barnabas reminded everyone how good God was and what his grace and power were like close to hand.

James concluded by saying that it was all there in the Bible anyway: cultures and backgrounds all coming to know God through the Messiah in their own language and culture. James recommended that the church should not make it difficult for Gentiles who decide to follow Christ. Guidelines were proposed by James, agreed by a clear majority.

A letter for the church in Antioch was drafted according to James' proposal and is attached.

Any Other Business: travel arrangements for Paul, Barnabas, Judas and Silas were agreed and a token of appreciation from the churches of Judea bought in response to the kind financial support from Antioch during the famine.

SOUNDTRACK 🎧

Prepare a time of prayer and personal devotion, paying particular attention to the senses. Play some meditative music, something which helps you focus and is not a distraction. Light a scented candle or joss stick. Find a smooth pebble or stone. Fill a small saucer with honey. Use your senses to thank God and worship the Creator:

Creator God
Breathe your Spirit into me as I breathe this incense
Bring your mercy and forgiveness as I taste this sweetness
Speak your words to me as I am surrounded by this music
Be my rock as I touch this stone
Amen

TAKEAWAY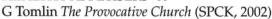

Reflecting on the journey of Kumar, are there Christians you know from another faith background? If you have never found out their story, do so now. Take time listening to them. What were their struggles? How has church life been for them?

Research the rich resources of non-Western Christian theologians and spiritual leaders. If you do not know where to start, try an Internet search of people such as Sadhu Sundar Singh, Vinoth Ramachandra, Lamin Sanneh, Rene Padilla or Kosuke Koyama. Read about their lives and their spirituality. Reflect on the different and surprising perspectives they bring.

BANQUET

M Volf *Exclusion and Embrace: A Theological Exploration of Identity, Otherness, and Reconciliation* (Abingdon Press, 1996)

HEALTHY APPETISERS

G Tomlin *The Provocative Church* (SPCK, 2002)
See http://www.baptist.org.uk/resources/inclusivity_resources. asp?section=21 to order the following resources:
Many Nations One Church – study guide produced in conjunction with Christian Aid containing challenging questions to help churches move in the direction of God's plan for a new humanity that will embrace all nations.
We Belong – an ecumenical racial justice starter training pack, celebrating cultural diversity and living hospitality.

VIRTUAL FOOD

See resources informing a church that embraces a fusion of east and west cultures, http://eastandwest.co.uk/sanctuary.html
Worship music reflecting South Asian spirituality and DVDs with alternative worship meditations and visuals are available to order on this site.

Chapter 9

Fuel for the Journey: Spirituality for Interfaith Work

'In my songs, the verse is the blues, the chorus is the gospel.
The grit, then the prayer. To me, that's life'.   Bruce Springsteen

I hope that by now you've detected the enthusiasm and commitment to ministry among people of other faiths which this book represents. I'm harbouring a secret ambition that this material will not just offer some guidelines and encouragements to those already involved. I'd love to see a new generation of Christians feel called to mission and ministry in a context of religious diversity. But I'd be offering only a partial picture if that message did not come with a caution. This chapter, then, aims to go back to the source and remind us of what roots and sustains us as Christians in a changing and challenging world.

There's a large sign posted over a buoy in the harbour of Port Talbot, South Wales, declaring, *'Do not anchor between signs'*. The boats are meant to keep moving between the buoys in the harbour and can only settle when they have clear instructions to do so. It's a neat illustration for me of the need for us to be hearing from God in what are the busy and treacherous waters of multi-faith Britain. We dare not stay in a place where *all* we are doing is community service or dialogue or even evangelism. These are not endpoints for Christians and the church. Our worship of God is an endpoint. Now, contrary to my natural inclination to activity and achievement, I've repeatedly had to remind myself that God does not, first and foremost, require my activity. It's sobering to recognise that even Jesus did not have a Messiah complex, and neither should we. As it says in that foundational statement in the Westminster Shorter Catechism: 'The chief end (ie purpose) of man (humankind) is to glorify God and enjoy him forever'.

Our evangelism, community action, youth projects, even our churches, will all pass away. Communion with Father God, in contrast, will never end. God delights to be with us, and if we neglect the cultivation of our worship, praise, prayer and Bible reading, the foundations of the new creation which we build in our acts of service are in danger of becoming monuments to our own endeavour.

In one sense, this chapter is like one of those signs in the harbour at Port Talbot: spend a little time here before moving on. Whatever your engagement with other faiths, never forget to come back to the still point: the marker of God's presence and blessing for you and your Christian community. This might seem an obvious point and one that is relevant to all our lives. That would be true. But there are some special considerations when we encounter convictions of faith. As I write this, I'm wrestling with what terms to use, conscious of the various bits of baggage Christian jargon brings with it. The nature of Christian life and witness in a plural society is one that is charged with the character of spiritual warfare. Now, spiritual warfare – there's another dreaded term which I'm going to attempt to redeem! That phrase may get your adrenaline pumping as you excitedly contemplate a call to arms or, alternatively, it might leave your blood running cold, worried that this book is suddenly defaulting to lazy stereotypes. You may be just intrigued as to where I'm going next! But stay with me.

People of other faiths are often very clear about what they believe. Many derive a great solace and strength of communal identity from their faith. This should not be a surprise to us. As we interact with other faiths, then, we need to be especially conscious of who *we* are. This has been implicit in the idea of distinctive faith, because the pattern of our engagement is shaped by foundational Christian concepts. But the reality of a distinctive faith is not worked out primarily in training manuals, seminars and programmes. Rather, distinctive faith becomes embedded when we pray in community, read our Scriptures and look to our Christian story.

We can see the pattern of Jesus' life modelling this for us in his encounter with *our* difference! I don't know whether you've recognised the two special moments that publicly proclaimed Jesus' identity: his baptism and transfiguration. They are like bookends to his earthly ministry. In Matthew 3, a voice declares over Jesus, as he is baptised by John, 'This is my Son, whom I love; with whom I am well pleased.'. Immediately after the baptism, Jesus is drawn out into the desert to fast for 40 days and is tempted by the devil, prior to any preaching and healing. In Matthew 17, the disciples witness Jesus transfigured, with Moses and Elijah beside him, and a voice calls out, 'This is my Son, whom I love; with whom I am well pleased.' Resisting Peter's wish to start a Christian festival at the site of the Transfiguration, Jesus talks about the path of suffering ahead as he sets his face toward Jerusalem and the cross. Those two bookends also offer a cameo of the baptism that is death and the Transfiguration that is resurrection life and glory.

Throughout the Gospels, Jesus is presented as a man with a clear sense of who he is and what he is called to do. A million and one agendas are imposed upon him; a myriad labels, ambitions and boxes to frame him. And none of them fits. Jesus resists them all and as the intensity of the opposition to his words and actions increases, so does Jesus' singular focus on the destination of the cross. Right at the end, while the disciples are still enjoying an adventure of missing the point and arguing about who is the greatest, Jesus takes his outer robes off and washes their feet. How can Jesus do this? John tells us: 'Jesus knew that the Father had put all things under his power, and that he had come from God and was returning to God, so he got up from the meal, took off his outer clothing, and wrapped a towel round his waist' (John 13:3,4). Jesus knew his source, his identity and his ultimate destiny.

Jesus engaged with a context brimful of different versions of the good life. You could have your religion Pharisee-style, Sadducee-like or Essene. Throw in the idolatries of the ruling Romans, the syncretism of the Samaritans or the pic'n'mix of the collaborators and you had yourself a heady cocktail. There was religion for the hardcore, mystical, revolutionary, pietist or nominal; and every variation in between. And there was plenty of need to be going along with communities of people with leprosy, the sick and the lame in every village, the poor and the disenfranchised from the oppressive rule of the Romans. Did Jesus meet all the needs or fit any of the programmes and agendas imposed upon him? No. We have accounts of Jesus moving away from villages whose people beseeched him to stay, to teach and to heal more of the sick.

Always, as Jesus served, and his sense of identity was by no means removed from the hard realities of suffering, he knew who he was and what he was called to be and do.

We live in an age of such competing identities and need. A spirituality which can stay true to God's calling to each of us is vital. And remember those bookends? The devil in the desert is keen to push another way of being and doing on to Jesus: 'try the quick fix, Jesus,' 'the shortcut to popularity', 'the easily digestible alternative'. After the Transfiguration, the devil speaks through Peter: 'Hey, this is what it's all about: let's just run a 24 hour bless-up meeting'. In both cases, Jesus has set his goals on a destination not visible to anyone else. Jesus has spent time finding out what God really wants of him. The route to the destination is no cosy option, either; it will bring with it considerable pain and suffering. But the journey is possible because God has mapped it out and God will be there every step of the way, blessing and affirming.

It is something of this identity and purpose that we must retain and consolidate as we engage with other faiths. Before I unpack this, let me provide a qualification crucial to how we view the spiritual struggle with which we are *all* involved. I hear lots of talk from Christians who believe there is something intrinsically dangerous and hostile within the practice of other faiths. My friend and co-worker Andrew Smith, on encountering similar attitudes, likes to pose a question: 'Now how many of you know Christian friends who have converted to another faith? OK. . . Now how many of you know Christian friends who have drifted away to secularism and do not believe *anything* any more?' The chances are that the latter situation is the more familiar to people. The conclusion? Are we as determined to protect and guard ourselves when we are shopping in malls or drinking in the local bar and club? These are equally contexts where our Christian identity and calling will be challenged, where there is a struggle for our very being. The messages of what the good life may be might not come with faith labels. But the scripts and texts of a very powerful alternative to the gospel are being written and learned in a multitude of ways: *Just do it*, *Because you're worth it*, *The Real Thing*. These are not bland and valueless pieces of the jigsaw of contemporary life, the obviously religious pieces carrying the real threat. These slogans offer corrosive challenges to a distinctive Christian faith.

There is a right and proper suspicion of relationships with other faiths which results in syncretism: a merging of faiths into a hybrid which somehow betrays both. But I rarely hear warnings about the syncretism practised daily by so many of us Christians. We readily fit our gospel of good news into a package which justifies and perpetuates living in the best neighbourhoods, with the nicest houses and the exotic holidays and schools that are 'just-so'. And we forget that our lives should be shaped by the good news rather than the gospel being squeezed into a part of our lives. We all live with this ambiguity, and I don't want to start a guilt trip but rather to prod us to consider the backdrop of the true nature of the spiritual struggle. Who are we? What are we called to do and become? Where are we going? . . . Whoever we are, these questions are vital for Christians to keep asking themselves in a plural world.

I'd like to offer a few guidelines for keeping on track; being true to ourselves in the complexity and challenge of plurality. These guidelines are about rooting ourselves in the Christian story. They are significant in placing our present in the context of a past and a future. It's been said that history is 'what happens to other people at another time in another place.' When we become Christians, we don't inherit just a history, we inherit a *memory*. The stories of the people of Israel, of the disciples and of the early church, become *our* stories. This is something intrinsic to Jewish spirituality, typically in the celebration of the Passover, the liberation by God of the Jews from Egypt. The youngest Jewish family member will ask of the oldest, 'Tell us what it was like for us in Egypt.' The history becomes a tangible memory as they recall God's love and power at work. Similarly, a Christian identity draws from the memory of that story but supremely in the story of the cross and resurrection of Jesus. That pivotal event in history becomes the place where *we* betray, *we* deny, but then are forgiven and given new life.

And it doesn't stop there, because there is a future and a hope. In the promise of the Holy Spirit, we have a cash advance of the abundance of God's kingdom that is 'already and not yet.' There is something inherently incomplete and provisional about all that we know and experience. In a sense, the church is to be an anticipation or advance guard of what is to come; not pointing to itself, but to a new creation centred on Christ. So we live with a rich and defining memory that shapes our present towards a future that is to come. . . And come it will! At a fundamental level, we might even say that our ability to relate effectively to others who are different, is dependent upon our ability be clear about our own story. Perhaps, to accept others, we need to be able to accept ourselves first.

When Jesus encourages his disciples to 'remember' him in the bread and wine of that Last Supper, the new Passover for Christians, we have some clues about how we might root ourselves in the memory and future of Jesus. Whether we name this practice Holy Communion, the Eucharist or the Breaking of Bread is not important. What is significant is the naming and blessing with which God charges us at those marker points in our journey.

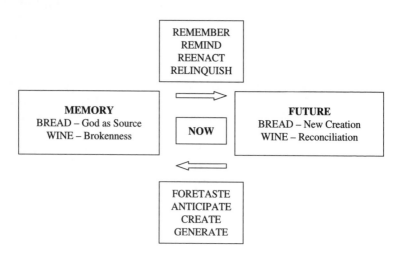

Offering a distinctive faith in a world of difference, we need to live in the 'present' in such a way as to draw from a reservoir of memory and celebrate a future. To some extent, this chapter is about what we do and say as Christians with each other in order that we have anything worth doing and saying to people of other faiths. How do we repeatedly tell our story amongst ourselves in a way that fuels our story in the wider world? What Christian disciplines keep us distinctive and sustain the authentic witness, dialogue and community service that we have articulated throughout this book?

1. MEMORY

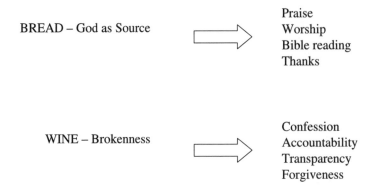

BREAD – God as Source

Praise
Worship
Bible reading
Thanks

WINE – Brokenness

Confession
Accountability
Transparency
Forgiveness

BREAD

As we remember how dependent we are upon God, how he provides for us and loves us, we are bound to respond in thankfulness and worship. In fact, the practice of praise becomes a reminder of our dependency upon God. Part of that provision is in the bread of the scriptures and the feeding on the story that we own. There will be the formal liturgies of some traditions, crafted words punctuating our worship or the informal liturgies of exuberant praise. Whatever our denomination or brand of Christianity, without exception, a practice of our dependency upon God is a springboard to a distinctive faith which engages with the world. So, we *remember* God's goodness, *remind* each other of his love and *re-enact* the Last Supper to draw on the promise of the presence of God from whom all good things come. As we feed on the bread, we *relinquish* our claims to independence from God.

WINE

The wine is a vivid picture of our brokenness, a reminder of God's judgement and the suffering of the world. This is not to be baulked at but to be embraced. Again, whether we have formal times of confession in our respective traditions is less important than the periodic practice of recalling that we mess up, continue to fail and are utterly dependent on God's grace. A memory of brokenness demands truthfulness in relationship and drives us to accountability, transparency and the practice of forgiveness. We *remember* our weakness, *remind* each other of our need of forgiveness and *re-enact* the bitterness of acknowledging our part in continuing to fall short of God's requirements. As we drink the wine, we *relinquish* all pretence that we can please God from our own efforts.

In both our personal and communal lives as Christians, we need to foster a memory which glorifies God and underscores our humility. The counterpoint to this practice of memory is the celebration of the future:

2. FUTURE

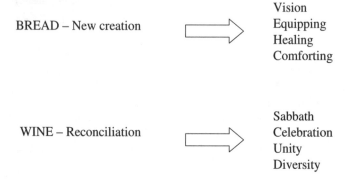

BREAD – New creation

Vision
Equipping
Healing
Comforting

WINE – Reconciliation

Sabbath
Celebration
Unity
Diversity

BREAD
While the bread is a picture that draws to the past of our own need and God's provision, it is also a symbol which sets our face forward to the future of the new creation. The meal we share is a foreshadowing of a great feast that is to come when all suffering will end, all tears be dried and God will dwell among his people. Our spirituality, then, needs to include a setting of vision, of what we can be and where we are heading as Christians and as a Church. We ain't seen nothing yet! So, teaching, preaching and discipling is not just about looking back to a shared memory but looking forward, with excitement and hope. The practice of gifts within the church to equip and build up people, and the healing and comforting which make the Christian community a place of peace provide tangible experiences of that future. Our end goal is not looking back to some idealised moment of the early church but a vision of the new

creation brought forward into the present. As Christians, our prayers, reading and worship need to include something of this dynamic of *Foretasting* and *Anticipating*. As we *Create* and *Generate* opportunities for new life and the redemption of people and places, Christians are offering glimpses of the kingdom of God here and now.

WINE
The wine is a picture of the glory and abundance of the kingdom of God; the richness of the feast. Resurrection life is a Sabbath of rest, a time when labours and struggles end and humanity will be at one with the Creator. The divisions between people and between people and God will be broken down, all made possible by the blood of Jesus. So in the book of Revelation, we have a window into a community of diversity and unity centred around Christ, with no walls, no impediments, in full celebration and praise. Our spirituality should be able to foster *foretastes* and *anticipations* of this diversity and unity. Prayer and worship ought to include the *creation* and *generation* of celebration, rest and hope.

Christians are a people with a memory and a future. Staying true in our spirituality to this tension will help us stay true to our identity as Christians, enabling us to be the distinctly welcoming people we are called to be in a multi-faith world.

I think I understand you. I need to have a closer look at that diagram, but you seem to be saying that we need a balance in our spirituality. What I can't quite get my head around is why make such a deal about this in a book looking at other faiths. Surely, this is material for a book on Christian Spirituality?

To some extent, that's true. The pointers that I've provided are relevant to every one of us. But I think there are some particular issues that come up with other faiths that relate to these guidelines. The sense of 'balance' is crucial because it is so easy to get sucked into a spirituality that is one-dimensional. So, if all you do is beat yourself up about how terrible you have been and how you are dependent upon God and His forgiveness, you are in danger of forgetting that you are a new creation and God has given you

His spirit to transform your life and the lives of others. If you bring such an imbalance to a person confident about their own faith, you might have a tendency to always criticise Christians and the church, and forget the challenge that the church brings to others. Or you might emphasise so much the victory of Jesus, and the celebration of the life to come that you forget the humility that comes of remembering our brokenness. When engaging with other faiths, an overly triumphalistic approach can be especially hollow sounding to those who remember only too well the wrongs the church has committed in the past.

Here are a few specific applications of a rounded spirituality which is up to the task of interacting with other faiths.

Christians with a memory and a future. . .

– will not be panicked by feeling like a small vulnerable minority because God has provided and sustained and is bringing all his people together into a new creation.
– will always present hope, even in the midst of conflict and bad news, because God is making all things new.
– will avoid judging other groups and individuals without first judging themselves because the grace on which we are dependent is part of our memory.
– will never be satisfied with the *status quo*, about what is "good enough", because they will be restlessly searching for and enabling God's future.
– will always have enough, even when resources are stretched and seemingly insufficient, because they take time to rest in the Sabbath of God's presence.
– will delight in the gifts which Christians bring from all sorts of cultures, traditions and ages because these are signs of God's creativity and abundance which will be fully evident in the new creation.
– will have not be afraid of a future which seems to push the church to the margins, knowing that God brings his new creation in the vulnerability of a slain lamb.

The process of praying, reading, worshipping in this manner is not a static one. We need to bring our experiences of interaction with other faiths into our personal and communal times of worship. We also need to take what we hear in these times of worship into fresh encounters. That's why this book has been structured as it has. I've wanted there to be something of this model exemplified. Reflecting on the Bible, praying and worshipping, taking the other-faith encounter seriously and working out what this means for our lifestyles: this is a cycle that ought to be the norm. The creative Bible reflections have not been intended as a kind of gimmick to offer a quirky angle on Scripture. No, I believe there is a desperate need for us to be rooting the Bible in our own experiences, being true to its message and context but striving to see how it may point to our own lives so that we release more of its authority. If you have a friend who is a Sikh or have befriended a Hindu in your local youth project, whatever your situation, dig deep into those conversations and encounters in prayer and worship to listen to what God may be saying to you. Our call to be a distinctive people of Christ can only be sustained when we underpin our relationships and projects with a spirituality equal to them.

It seems appropriate to conclude this chapter with some 'Top Tips' for a Christian spirituality for interfaith relationships:

- keep asking yourself, 'What does God want to teach *me* through this relationship, encounter and project?'
- read the Bible through the lens of a multi-faith world.
- read the full breadth of the Bible. Not just the gospels or the epistles! Our memory and future becomes rounded in the fullness of what there is in the Bible.
- ask for discernment about your own journey alongside people of other faiths. There are religious practices which God forbids and which have spiritual potency and danger. There are some which are just empty and futile. And there are those which are a genuine reaching out and searching for God. Be conscious of listening to God about these differences.
- keep in Christian community. No Christian spirituality fosters an island mentality. Bring your prayers and worship with others who are similarly engaged; bring those questions and checks and balances to each other.
- in community, help each other not to get too cocky and triumphant . . . But also ensure that you don't perpetuate a doormat mentality. You have a future and a hope!

- listen to the promptings of God's Spirit: when might it be right to speak out and explain the hope you bear or to challenge something in the person or institution of another faith?
- listen to the promptings of God's Spirit: when might you be hearing God speaking to you through the voice of a person of another faith?
- make times for celebration and thanks, for good food and laughter. This is part of our spirituality and a taster of what is to come. It should never be about earnest drudgery!

A LA CARTE 🍽️ – Ephesians 6:10-20

Some final advice: be a muscular Christian. No, not from your own ability, will power or strength. The kind of training and exercise you need doesn't happen in a gym. Get your energy from God instead then you'll be really up for the fight ahead. Put on every bit of the armour of God; all that makes you who you are in Christ. Let it be like clothing to you, protecting you, keeping you warm, being visible to all. By wearing God's armour, you'll be distinctively Christian and be able to withstand all the schemes of the devil.

Remember, our enemies are not Hindus, Muslims, Sikhs, Buddhists or Secularists. Our struggle is against the sin and brokenness which locks and binds people into slavery of all kinds. This kind of slavery is evil; it has spiritual force and can only be unlocked by lives lived in the Spirit. God's armour is like a second skin to those who make a difference in the battle in which we are engaged. If you take this stuff seriously, when tough times come, you know who you are, who is looking over you, where your real energy and identity comes from. You'll not be fazed by confusing ideas, alternative spiritualities and the kind of religion that's based on an endless determination to do better. You will be able to stay 'in the zone': the zone of God's protection and purpose. And when you have done what God has called you to do, you'll not be floundering, exhausted, looking for the next spiritual high. You'll stay true to who you are in Christ: a child loved, accepted with a future and a hope. Earthly battles are high-octane affairs, lots of action and immense busyness. God's warriors are a still point in a confusing and bewildering world: secure, confident and at peace.

Be rooted in Christ.

Speak truth about people of other faiths; don't generalise or stereotype but only say what you know is true. Be true to who you are, too. It might mean you are not always popular with everyone. So speak out against sin and injustice and do not be ashamed of Christ and the reason for your hope. Be truthful in your words and deeds and it will be like a belt holding you in the fight.

Hunger after pure behaviour and it will be like a breastplate covering your heart. Have pure motives, clear agendas and honest relationships with people of other faiths. These should be core to who you are.

Look for every opportunity to offer peace and be a person of peace. To do this, you need to be ready at a moment's notice to respond to what is happening around you: it will be like the wearing of shoes which don't bog you down in the battlefield. In a world of religious conflict, take each chance that comes to be good news even when religion just seems to be bad news.

Attacks will come from all sorts of unforeseen angles. Remember, it's really Satan who is attacking you, so have God's perspective on your situation. God is victorious and is bringing his new creation; never forget this even when there are few signs of newness. This will be your shield against the attacks and will help you to persevere: this is not the end!

Don't forget that you are forgiven and you have assurance of new life with God! When you are following God in a multi-faith world, the central fact of what Jesus has done for you on the cross should never be lost. Lose that conviction and you may as well go into a battle without a helmet; you'll be dead in minutes!

And your weapons aren't clever arguments, manipulative sermons or intimidating threats. Your sword is the Bible. It contains a past and a future, a story which includes you. It's not your sword, though. It's not a book that is just read and learnt like any other. This book becomes a weapon in the battle only when God breathes his life into it. So pray! Keep praying! Keep asking for help! Sometimes we won't know what to ask for and we'll be out of our depth. But in those moments, we're thrown right on God's grace and power because this kind of battle isn't about physical stamina but about dependence on God. This means that we can't do this on our own. Pray those prayers for Christians everywhere! In the inner cities, in the suburbs. In universities and schools, in the countryside. In community churches, Baptist churches, Anglican churches, Black Majority churches, Roman Catholic churches and Methodist churches. In Britain, continental Europe, Africa, Asia, South America. Remember that we're all part of the same family, called to make a difference in a world of difference.

SOUNDTRACK 🎧

Write your spiritual journey. This can be in the form of a memoir or it could be in diagrammatic form. Take to time to remember the most significant times of your journey to and with Christ. What events, people and situations were instrumental in your story? What events, people and situations have helped shaped your understanding of Jesus since you have become a Christian? Thank God for these memories; your story. Ask God to speak to you about where this story might be going: what might God be challenging you about and what new discoveries may be ahead?

TAKEAWAY

Reflect on the 'Top Tips' above. If you have friends of other faiths or are involved in a project relating to other faiths, consider how you might incorporate these tips into your relationship and practice. For example, do you need to make intentional space to pray with other Christians and bring the learning and challenges of encounters into your worship experience? What about your Bible reading? Have you made efforts to reflect on Scripture in a multi-faith context? Pray about all this and make some commitments to developing your spirituality appropriately.

BANQUET

S Wells *God's Companions: Reimagining Christian Ethics* (Blackwell Publishing 2006)

HEALTHY APPETISERS

J Ortberg *The Life You've Always Wanted: Spiritual Disciplines for Ordinary People* (Zondervan, 2004)

VIRTUAL FOOD

The *Re:Jesus* site, http://www.rejesus.co.uk/ offers creative perspectives on Jesus and spirituality with online prayers and meditations

Follow an interactive model of Christian prayer through the *Labyrinth*, http://web.ukonline.co.uk/paradigm/

Explore resources and tips for worship relevant to contemporary culture at http://www.alternativeworship.org/

Chapter 10

My Space? Embracing a Post-Christian Society

'It was really hard; it was like being abroad'.   Ian Rush

Back in the 1980s when footballers wore mullet haircuts and ridiculously tight shorts, the Liverpool and Wales striker, Ian Rush, spent a disastrous year playing for Juventus in the Italian league. Interviewed on his return home, he was famously quoted as saying, 'It was really hard; it was like being abroad'. Now we don't necessarily expect the greatest insight from footballers but I do wonder whether Christians suffer from a similar sense of disorientation.

In Britain, we're used to churches in every town, Christian festivals celebrated, nativity plays wept over and weddings made complete in Christian liturgy and sacred space. We even have a state church, and the Queen, at least in legal terms, can choose the Archbishop. OK, we realise that all those things and more are not quite as they used to be. People hold loosely to them; there's a lot of form that masquerades as spirituality and, let's be honest, for the majority most of our Christian festivals are generally just a good excuse for a party. The challenge is to be able to distinguish between the practices of the Christian faith which are properly part of British society and those which are vestiges of privilege and power and are what we might term aspects of 'Christendom'.

All those trappings which we might call Christendom make it exceedingly difficult for us truly to envisage the proper place of the church in society. The church in Britain no longer commands a seat around the table in the cultural and moral life of the nation. The past is indeed like another country: people do things differently there.

Ever so slowly, we are beginning to work out some of the things we need to do differently. The whole fresh expressions/mission-shaped/emerging church movement conversation is just one aspect of this transition. No longer can we assume that people will come to the church for advice, counsel, moral guidance and pastoral support. We have to do the moving!

I don't know whether you've heard stories of missionaries trying to find language to connect with the Bible story in their cultural context. Tribes which have no word for "sin" or "heaven" provide a knotty challenge for Bible translators to find an equivalent dynamic which conveys the essence of the original concept. Or, how do you translate 'your sins will be as white as snow' to a people who do not know what snow is? I believe that this translation problem faces us in the church now in Britain. The 'translation' we are talking about is not merely linguistic but cultural. You may be picking up on the fact that many of the principles proposed within this book are applicable not just to working with other faiths but to anyone. But once again, these principles are sharpened when we consider our other faith neighbours.

For this to become clearer, we need to take a step back and study a little history. No relationship occurs in a vacuum and, whether we like it or not, history has a legacy which informs the present, shaping expectations, hopes, language and how we interpret each other. If I were to come home with a bunch of flowers, you may conclude that I am offering a sign of love to my wife and that I am an incurable romantic. If my wife and I had had a blazing row that morning, *we* may understand the gift of flowers as a peace offering or a demonstration of an apology. If my wife had given me the flowers that morning and then we had had the blazing row on the telephone during the day, we may interpret the return of the bouquet as my rejection of her gift and my continued anger. We all have a history! The trouble for us as churches is often our selective memory, ironing out some of the stories which continue to shape our engagement with wider society and especially those of other faiths.

The history of many of our other faith neighbours emanates from a story of British wealth and Empire. This Empire was conspicuously Christian but often not very Christ-like in its exploitation and racism. From the 1940s onwards, as the Empire began to crumble, the British dependence on resources from its colonies continued in a fresh form with the influx of labour from South Asia and the Caribbean, in particular. Our shared history reminds us that the welcome received by many of the immigrants was far from warm, in every respect. The story continues today with the lukewarm 'welcome' to asylum seekers and Eastern European migrant workers. Britain, this powerful and rich nation, uses and sometimes abuses the foreign and the different. Overlay this story with an association between Britain and Christianity, and the strangeness of religious and cultural difference brought by so many of the South Asian, Somali, Turkish, Iraqi and Iranian communities, and there is huge scope for misunderstanding.

It's easy to say, 'But we know most of this country's people are *not* Christian! *We* are the minority now'. This is true. The challenge is to demonstrate that we are not defaulting back into relationships which are abusive and underpinned by power and privilege. How can the church relate to those of other faiths in such a way as to *prove* the loving, wooing, serving nature of the good news of Christ? While working in North Africa, I was constantly amazed by the number of times the Crusades came up in conversation from Muslims. The feelings of suspicion and alienation from Christian symbols associated with aggression and imperialism were so tangible that it seemed that Richard the Lionheart had died only recently. For many Indian Hindus, there is a very painful legacy from missionary efforts which often sought to negate and demonise the cultural heritage of Indians, anglicising as they Christianised. Today, that can be felt in deep sensitivity to Christians who clumsily present the West as the norm for values of freedom, justice and godliness.

> *'Love is not a victory march,*
> *It's a cold and it's a broken Hallelujah'.*
> Leonard Cohen

Recognising that we are not a Christian country means appreciating, too, that many of our other faith neighbours will have more in common with sincere followers of Christ than will our secular, consumerist neighbours. The individualism fostered by the Big Brother world of celebrity and its worship of beauty, sex and money should be abhorrent to a faithful Christian discipleship. We are not at home here! Rather, when we notice the interdependence of other faith communities, and frequently their strong sense of family or respect for the elderly, we are reminded that we need to sift out Christian values from supposedly British values and rediscover how the gospel affirms and challenges *all* cultures.

145

Let's look at three arenas where the Christendom/post-Christendom tension is played out specifically with regard to those of other faiths.

TERRITORY

A colleague of mine has developed a neat case study to generate discussions about Christian attitudes to other religions among us. He paints a scenario of a church struggling with finances, with an attached but under-used church hall. The local mosque/temple/gurdwara (pick your relevant place of worship!) sees this largely vacant church hall and believes it to be an ideal site for their expansion plans. You are on the team of church elders, parish church council, trustees of the building: what do you do? The money from the purchase could pay for the restoration of the church building, towards a youth worker, or for a new missions project. And as in all good case studies, you *have* to make a choice!

How do we view our territory, whether it be specifically the 'church' or our neighbourhood? Is it ours? Is it 'Christian'? What is the biblical view of our connection to the space we live in? These are massive questions (I won't attempt to answer here, you'll be relieved to know) and they are particularly pertinent ones in our inner cities where such scenarios are more than merely abstract discussion starters. The beauty of the case study is that while groups agonise, within a time-limit, over their decision, the facilitator throws in something from left field: 'Hold on everyone! We have some good news. At the last minute, a betting agency has offered to purchase the church hall. You have another option available. What do you do now?'

It's a delicious dilemma and sums up, in microcosm, the probing questions asked by our multi-faith context of the heart of the Christian faith. Would we rather have a betting shop in the church hall or a mosque? I won't give you my answer to the dilemma because there is no neat and clear-cut response. Rather, our motives, our calling, the specific missionary task of each church, our integrity, our relationships and, underlying it all, our appreciation of the breadth of God's work in our society, are all probed by such an issue. You see, Christendom tends to view patches of land (countries, neighbourhoods, continents) as under the ownership of a religion. The kingdom of God, which has designs on the whole cosmos, is breaking through in and beyond our churches, in surprising and wonderful places and cannot be ring-fenced. It's this *missio dei* stuff again.

Where would Jesus have spent his time in that case study? It's a mischievous question, because Jesus would have been praying in the church, discussing texts with the mosque/temple/gurdwara leaders and joking with those having a flutter on the horses. The hard boundaries which people erect around their own castles mean nothing to the border-crossing God who brings his life and love into all places.

When you view religion as a label for some territory, following that religion becomes the simple task of following the dominant values of that patch of territory. So, for hundreds of years, being British meant that you were a 'Christian'. By inference, being a white person, christened as an infant, married in a church and otherwise being a loyal Christian citizen seemed, for so many, to be the sum of allegiance to Christ. That's certainly how many of our other faith neighbours and other nations, view us. When religion is separated from territory, a vital witness and allegiance to the God who breaks all boundaries is possible. He is the God who crosses all borders and whose life bursts through the darkness without and within. Discipleship in this dispensation is genuinely costly but the route to faithful obedience is more starkly outlined than in a context of privatised nominalism.

So should I not be concerned that I see churches converted into temples, and that we seem to be losing our grip on what was once a Christian nation?

I'm not going to give a clear answer to that question either. It depends! It's heartbreaking to see the decline of the church in Britain. There is a genuine grief necessary to our embrace of the fact of being a post-Christian nation. Appreciating history means acknowledging that, in many ways, things are harder for Christians and we have lost so much. However, when we become exercised by the growth of other faiths in our country, are we as troubled by the rampant consumerism of the majority secular society? If all that remains of our Christian witness is the remnant of a building with a spire and a cross, is that particular witness what we should be grieving over? Or should we be more disturbed by the drift of Christians from poorer communities (where we find the majority of our other-faith neighbours!) into affluent suburbs?

BLESSING OUR CITIES – Jeremiah has to be my favourite prophet. I think there is a personality type connection going on here because, (yet another confession!), I'm often drawn to the miserable anti-hero. Not for me the glamorous, frothy heroism of James Bond or Tom Cruise in the *Mission Impossible* series. Give me Gene Hackman in a pork-pie hat, the outsider pushing against the system, tortured and fragile but bringing a peculiar transformation. That's what you get in spades with Jeremiah. Just when you think it's all going to come good for him, he's out of prison, and wham, he's thrown into the bottom of a cistern. Oh, and the cistern has no water in it so he is up to his waist in mud. God's servant had the worst job description going.

You see, God called Jeremiah to speak and embody a message which was as uncomfortable for his hearers as it was for him. Israel had become too much at ease with its status of being chosen and set apart by God. The ritual had become a Sabbath-only rite to tick the box of God's blessing. For the rest of the week, it was big business as usual and dalliance with whatever religion would ease the pain, fill the void and satisfy the desires. Trouble was coming in the form of a Babylonian army waiting outside the city and no one, but no one, was going to rescue them this time. No invisible angels, no pocket armies, no miraculous wave, because God was behind the impending upheaval.

However, God still had plans for the city and his people. The trouble was, Israel's plans looked considerably different from God's. And this is the bit I love: God told Jeremiah, who had spent all that time announcing the bad news of invasion and conquest, to buy a vineyard. How would you have reacted to this? I know what I would have said: 'Hold on, God. I'm up to my ears in mud. It stinks here. I've been beaten, tortured, arrested, put in prison all because you told me to announce to everyone in Jerusalem that this place is history! All our wealth, all our land is under a compulsory purchase order with zero compensation. And with the little money I have left, you are expecting me to pay a price for something I might never enjoy in my lifetime. In fact, the chances are that some Babylonian will convert this beautiful vineyard into a pig farm or a place for idols.'

> 'The large print giveth and the small print taketh away'.
> Tom Waits

We don't get to hear whether Jeremiah did ask this kind of question; he just buys the vineyard. What's more, we never know what happens to the land either. The great lesson, though, is Jeremiah's costly investment in the future of the city. Not for his own gain or even for the gain of his own people but purely in obedience to God's call, something of the Kingdom, and ultimately of Christ, was illustrated, modelled and experienced in that simple purchase. A time would come when freedom would be known and God would be near to all his followers. Jeremiah's investment was the most steady funds transfer you could imagine but it depended upon an obedience to God and a commitment to everyone who happened to be in the city.

In Jeremiah 29, you get a flash forward of the scene post-destruction. God's people have been displaced; they're hemmed in as a powerless minority surrounded by alien gods. And what does God command Jeremiah to say to the Israelite exiles? 'Seek the peace and prosperity of the city to which I have carried you into exile. Pray to the Lord for it, because if it prospers, you too will prosper.' (Jeremiah 29:7). The selfishness and complacency which led to exile would bring with it the challenge of being a blessing to the whole of the city: to stay true to God and to be good news to people of all faiths and none. This would be the true route to their own blessing.

When we prefer to collude with the gods of our age in cosseting ourselves with all the best that money can buy, surrounding ourselves with the certainty offered in communities of 'people like us', we are playing a dangerous game. The large print of brands pointing to the good life all carry with them a shelf life that is in contrast to the eternal value of kingdom ventures.

God has not given up on any place or with any people. God will use whom he chooses and will shape circumstances and history to challenge his own followers to be more fully Christ-like. As with God's original call to Abraham, which came with promise and blessing, in bold print it is affirmed that the blessing and promise we inherit as followers of Christ is intended for the benefit of the *whole of creation*.

The historian-sociologist Rodney Stark[1] wrote an incredible book on the reasons for the growth of the early church. Analysing

---

[1] *The Rise of Christianity*, Rodney Stark (HarperSanFrancisco, 1997)

contemporary historical records and archaeological data, Stark wanted to answer in very pragmatic terms the question of how a small Jewish sect could grow so quickly and generate such global tremors. He records how a series of virulent plagues wiped out whole towns in the Middle East at the time of the early church but that these strains of the plague were not fatal. What made the impact of the plague fatal was that those who were not contaminated would flee a town and leave the sick to die of starvation and malnutrition. Historical evidence demonstrates that when everyone else had left, small Christian communities stayed behind to nurse, feed and clean the sick, often at great danger to themselves. Those towns and villages survived, and, surprise, surprise, growing and influential church groups multiplied where such tangible witnessing was experienced.

I wonder if the current malaise of 'white-flight' is Britain's own plague? Inner cities are not mortally ill; they are not destined to die. But many Christians, fearful of the intimidating schools, threatening ethnic diversity and declining church confidence prefer the comfort and uniformity of the suburbs. I'm not sure that the comfort and uniformity of the suburbs will be with us for too much longer but can we re-imagine the impact of small, radical communities of Christ-followers in our cities today? Not there primarily to bless God's chosen ones, but to bless the whole city, the whole community; to serve without fear or favour, in Jesus' name, without the need of privilege, status, prestige and claims to territory.

RELIGION AND IDENTITY
One of the most distasteful by-products of a Christendom view of the world is the implicit view that *our* culture is somehow better than *their* culture. When we assume that Christian faith flows from a specific territory and that being British means being Christian, we are elevating British culture and repeating the worst of colonialism.

It's easy to fall into this trap and it requires us to be able to discern something of the complexity of our identities. I suspect that, as Christians, we should have a head start in beginning to grasp what this may mean in practice because the media get this wrong so frequently when they represent the Christian faith. Have you ever groaned as a Christian when a spokesperson has been chosen by television news to speak on behalf of 'Christians'? More often than not, the spokesperson is a middle-aged man from the established church speaking without enthusiasm and utterly incomprehensible to the majority. How do you feel if you are young, female, or a member of a new church? Or if you are part of Britain's fastest growing church groups, the Black majority churches of our cities? Or have you watched a TV drama where the sole Christian happens to be repressed, dowdy and legalistic? If you are like me, you feel that churches are often stereotyped and the complexity and diversity of the Christian faith woefully presented.

The same goes for other religions! Jesus' simple injunction to 'love your neighbour as yourself' demands that we see beyond the superficial labels, and do some extra work on understanding someone's relationship to their own faith. That's exactly what I would expect of others as they reflect on my faith. When religion is just a power play that expects everyone to 'be like us', you don't need to encounter real people with their cultures, histories, specific beliefs and spiritualities. God enters into relationship with who we are, listening to our heart-cries, diving deep into our stories. Let's do the same for our other-faith neighbours!

This means that we should be wary of labelling and making quick judgements. (I hope this sounds like the kind of advice Jesus was fond of giving!) Our Christian faith affects every area of our lives but it will be expressed in different ways depending on our roles, culture, context, experiences and relationships. The challenge is that the values worked out in all these spheres should be consistent and Christ-like. Let me give another example.

I develop resources for Christians attempting to understand and engage with those of other faiths. I'm also a dad. In the evening, when I read my children a bedtime story, I don't open up a Powerpoint presentation on other faiths. I am acting in two very different capacities then. However, I hope that my Christian faith infuses the way I love my children, encourage love of people of other faiths, listen to students or prioritise friendships and my family. When I am reading a bedtime story, I am still a consultant on other faiths, still an Englishman from Lancashire only just the right side of 40 years of age. All of these things and more affect what I bring to each situation, and each encounter and rôle will require the juggling of these identities. What I do and say will vary but what should be foundational for all that I do and say are my Christian faith and values.

As we encounter people of other faiths, it is vital that we see beyond the label 'Hindu', to see a 'mother' called Sarita. That we perceive further than 'Muslim', to a 'Somali' called Ahmed'. That we discover the 'hardworking student' Mohan in the 'Sikh' or the 'devoted husband' Ajahn in the 'Buddhist'. Ultimately, let us aim to find the friend in the person of another faith, as did Jesus, our pattern, model and source.

Let me offer a summary guide to a shift in thinking from Christendom to Post-Christendom that loves and serves other faiths:

- from loving and serving territory to loving and serving community
- from loving and serving just my people to loving and serving all peoples
- from loving and serving my culture to loving and serving all cultures
- from loving and serving religious labels to loving and serving in relationship
- from loving and serving power to loving and serving self-lessly

A LA CARTE 🍽 – Daniel 1[2]

Abednego's story:

There's this cheesy old pop song that my mum and dad and their friends sometimes sing: "By the rivers of Babylon, there we sat down, and there we wept when we remembered Zion. . .". I used to think it was so naff, but the other day I was thinking about the words; they were going around and around in my head and I could see that perhaps it was kinda poignant: all about your dreams coming crashing down, everything you thought was rock solid collapsing around you, and all you can do is fill a foreign river with your tears.

I guess I ought to tell you who I am, give you a bit of background. My name is, well was, Azariah, but nowadays I'm called Abednego. They take your land, they take your name. They are the Babylonians, the superpower of our time, invincible, kindly spreading their version of democracy and

---

[2] Published with the kind permission of the author, Richard Woods

civilisation across the known world, whether we want it or not. They say their rule will last for ever. My new friend Daniel does this sort of enigmatic spiritual smirk when he hears that. He is one hugely unusual and interesting guy and in a minute I'm going to tell you about this strange thing he did a couple of weeks ago, but first, some more about me.

It was just over a year ago that they invaded our land and carried a load of us into captivity in this weird place. And if I can try to see it from my parents' perspective, I guess it must be hard. For generations their culture and their theology had been telling them that they would be in the land of Canaan for ever, and that from an unbroken line of kings a Messiah would emerge, because God was their God and in total charge of human affairs. Well, that doesn't look so clever from here: no king, no land, no unbroken line to this glorious future they keep talking about. Everything you had always believed has been turned around, made to look daft. Readjusting can be so hard. Is it easier to keep believing in a God who is doing stuff you don't understand, or do you just stop believing and give up hope? You invest your life to follow this God, you do all your devotions, you take care not to covet your neighbour's ox and all that, and your God seems to walk out on you.

Well, you know, I don't quite see it that way. Captivity hasn't been too bad for me. First, apparently, I have the X factor. You see, what they did when we first arrived here is that they set up these massive auditions and they trawled through hundreds and hundreds of us young guys with Ashpenaz, Babylonia's answer to Simon Cowell, sending away heartbroken young guys on the grounds of them being too slow, too ugly, too uneducated. . .never believe them when they say boys don't cry. There are these great words in a writ-up I saw saying that they picked – get this – 'young men, without any physical defect, handsome, showing aptitude for every kind of learning, well informed, quick to understand. . .' Heaven only knows why they picked me. A Friday afternoon selection if ever there was one.

Two of my mates got picked, too. Hananiah, now called Shadrach and so relieved not to be called Hannah for short any more, and Mishael who became Meshach mainly because they can't say 'Mishael' round here.

Chalk and cheese. Shadrach is so laid back, he has no problems with any of this: he sees it as some sort of madly good university where you don't need a student loan, you don't have to eat junk food and you get all your wine for free. For Student's Union read King's Palace. Pure white marble and sweet, sweet incense instead of sticky floors and a vague smell of vomit. His first words to me when he got picked? Words, perhaps you are *thinking, of great spiritual insight? 'He shoots, he scores. This is cool, innit?'*

By contrast, Meshach could agonise for Israel. Like everything is a huge moral issue for him. He agonised over whether it was morally right even to join the king's palace, he agonised as to whether it was corrupting to learn the literature and language of a pagan culture, he agonised whether by taking a Babylonian name he was aiding and abetting the dilution of the differentiation of God's chosen people. Didn't stop him doing any of it, though, but God at least knew how traumatic it was for him. Lord, I can barely bring myself to eat these oysters, this dressed crab, this parma ham, and carpaccio of beef from the finest Babylonian cattle. I'm really suffering here. He's OK actually, and he, like me, like Shadrach, well we've been on an amazing emotional journey. . .not sure where it is taking us but I really don't want it to stop.

It all comes back to this guy Daniel. Cool guy, Daniel; knows his mind. And he, and he alone, when he sees this amazing food and all this vintage wine, knows it is not what he's going to do. He's made his promises to God, he is going to stick to our religious food rules and he's not going to cave in to pressure. He tells Ashpenaz this is what he is going to do and that's all there is to it. Me, Meshach and Shadrach: we're looking on aghast. Ashpenaz goes into melt-down. Big, big panic. 'Daniel, you can't decline all this good stuff, you will simply waste away. Cholesterol is good for you. And if you do, the king – hardly famed for his calm reflection – is quite up for a bit of summary execution. Put simply: you turn veggie, you start to look scrawny, and I'm a dead man walking.' But Daniel cuts a deal. A ten day trial, like those adverts where they split the screen in two. See who looks the best: the royal food eaters on the one side or the detox dieters on the other. And something inside us, you could say God, is stirring us as we watch, and we want to be part of this. Give us nothing but water and lots and lots of vegetables, too. Something about Daniel makes you want to do what he does. Makes you want to go out on a limb for God, take a few chances.

Ten days come, ten days go. Shadrach craving for meat, hallucinating about something called a full English. Meshach trying hard to look serene, Daniel actually looking serene. And me? Coping. Feeling good, in fact. And in our ten day inspection, we look good. Surprisingly good. God-making-us-look-good good.

So it's just water and vegetables for me from now on. . . great.

OK, I know it doesn't seem much: just taking a small stand really. Hardly the most painful sacrifice in the history of our nation; and I know it's not as if they're going to throw us into a blazing furnace or anything – these are, as they constantly tell us, civilised, sophisticated, modern people, but I tell you something. This first taste of standing right on the edge for God made me feel better, more at home, more secure than I've ever felt before, even when I was back in my homeland. Standing on the edge: I believe with all my heart that my God would catch me if I fell off the edge with his strong arms, but even if he didn't, I'd still go there for him.

SOUNDTRACK 🎧

Father God, give me something of your X-ray vision! I find it so easy to label people, and I am often afraid of what is strange and different. Lord God, thank you that you look into people's hearts. Help me to do that. Give me the wisdom and the knowledge to see the heart cries of some of my friends and neighbours, especially those with another faith. And Lord, I pray for my town, my city; everyone in it. Help me and my church to be a blessing to all, that a river of life will flow from this place and benefit people of all backgrounds, colours and religions. Amen.

TAKEAWAY 🏍

If there is another faith community in your town or city, consider approaching the leadership there and asking for topics for prayer. As a church, treat this seriously and pray for the requests shared by this other faith community. Seek to ask God's blessing on this group and follow up the results with them. Explain that as a Christian community, you are called by God to bless the whole city or town, and that that includes them.

BANQUET 🏠

D Smith *Mission After Christendom* (T & T Clark, 2002)

HEALTHY APPETISERS 🍎

M Frost and A Hirsch *The Shaping of Things to Come* (Hendrickson Publishers, 2003)
Alan Hirsch *The Forgotten Ways* (Brazos Press, 2007)
S Murray *Post-Christendom* (Paternoster Press, 2004)

VIRTUAL FOOD 🖱

Ekklesia promotes thinking around Christian witness in the public square with a special attention to the post-Christendom context, http://www.ekklesia.co.uk/.

The Gospel and Our Culture Network provides resources that develop the thinking of Lesslie Newbigin in promoting mission in a Western multicultural and multi-faith context, http://www.gospel-culture.org.uk/.

http://www.emergingchurch.info/ for stories of new forms of church in a post-Christendom context.

RUN: www.run.org.uk for resources equipping mission and ministry in a post-Christendom context.

Postscript

'I'm just smart enough to know how stupid I am.'
Joe Strummer

A distinctly welcoming Christian faith in a multi-faith Britain . . .
Mmm. We've a long way to go, haven't we? There's a lot of
baggage and history which makes this quite a tall order. When we
meet as Christians, people with a memory but energised by a
future, we have to acknowledge that we're far from the finished
article. We're work in progress made from damaged goods. But
this is also part of the beauty and hope of what it means to be
Christian. God, strangely, takes delight in working with people
such as you and me, people who regularly trip up, fall over, get it
wrong and miss the point. Cue: big sigh of relief! So let's own our
incompleteness, our partial knowledge, our squinting into the
sunlight on God's horizon.

We will continue to fail until Jesus returns and the fullness of
the new creation is around us. Jesus is our start and finish, beginning and end. With Jesus as our plumb line, our source and our
goal, Christians will constantly be offering both comfort and
challenge to people of other faiths. We may even find other faith
friends and neighbours challenging us in the life they see in Jesus!
Back in the 1940s, the Christian missionary E. Stanley Jones wrote
a biography of his friend, Mahatma Ghandi. Stanley Jones asked
Ghandi how the Christian faith could be so rooted in Indian
society that it wasn't a foreign, British import but a natural part
of the national life of the country. This is what Ghandi said: *'I
would suggest first of all that all of you Christians, missionaries and all,
begin to live more like Jesus Christ. Second, practise your religion
without adulterating or toning it down. Third, emphasise love and make*

it your working force, for love is central in Christianity. Fourth, study the non-Christian religions more sympathetically to find the good that is in them, so that you might have a more sympathetic approach to the people.'[1]

This is great advice! What might a fully naturalised British Christian faith look like for the twenty-first century? It would look very different, depending on the cultures, places and ages which represent the diverse church in our country. But a rooted Christian faith will be so conscious of its story and its identity that it will be a transforming agency of love which can see the good in other faiths and challenge sin, all in the name of Jesus. And as we worship Jesus, we find out more and more, like Paul who saw himself as the worst of sinners, how little we do know. Our words and actions become tempered with our own incompleteness; not strident and full of certainty but hopeful and expectant, full of love.

The Church of England has set up a project called 'Presence and Engagement' to help resource those churches facing a multi-faith context and to educate and equip the wider church to an other faith encounter. I love the project's title! You see, plenty of people are 'present' in our inner cities and elsewhere, living and working alongside other faith neighbours. Plenty of people 'engage' in multi-faith concerns through missionary support, letter writing or short-term projects for the inner cities or abroad. The truly precious commodity is that life and witness which is both present *and* engaged. Present to know what it is like to live in a Hindu neighbourhood, hear the struggles of a Muslim mum, gain the trust of a Sikh teenager; engaged so that acts of love and service and words of truth are offered to each of these people in the name of Jesus. This is not about being determined to ring-fence the last bastions of the church in the dwindling Christianity of our urban centres. Nor is it about satisfying the intellectual curiosity of monocultural suburbs. Being present and engaged in the mixed cultures of Britain is about discovering God's calling on the church for this day and age.

And this is for all of us! During the Cold War, the capitalist countries of the West and the Communist countries of the East attempted to draw boundaries round each other. The Iron and

---

[1] *Ghandi: Portrayal of a Friend*, E. Stanley Jones (Abingdon Classics, 1948)

Bamboo Curtains were a vain attempt to keep a capitalist-free zone, untainted by inequality and greed. It was like those zones set up during the Foot and Mouth crisis in 2001: '*cordon sanitaires*'. You know, 'here be dragons!' I have a sneaking feeling that some Christians would prefer a *cordon sanitaire* of Christianity in Britain, a place which didn't have to deal with the messiness of turbans, veils and gurus. But that zone doesn't exist. The question of how Christians are to live with other faiths is not for the specialist and the exotic few. This is a fundamental question for the whole church. Because in God's economy, the only *cordon sanitaire* is in Jesus and Jesus has this unseemly habit of breaking across those dirty lines and embracing those who are different: we know that because that is our story!

We must never forget, too, that our call to be present and engaged means that Christians must stay present and engaged with God. We're good at being 'present' in worship, Bible reading and prayer but are we 'engaging': grappling with God over what he is saying to us in our specific situations or through our other faith encounters. Or we may be engaged with God very specifically over scriptures which help and inform our ministry but neglect to nurture simple rhythms of prayer and worship which give our spirituality the bigger picture. Being present and engaged with God is like a constant health check-up: looking for those vital signs and indicators, reviewing our diet and exercise.

We've already looked at Paul's famous speech in Athens in Acts 17. He says in that sermon, 'From one man he made every nation of men, that they should inhabit the whole earth; and he determined the times set for them and the exact places where they should live.' Do you ever feel that God has been looking elsewhere while mosques, gurdwaras and temples were being built over the last 40 years? Paul clearly had to overcome some strong personal reactions as he saw the various religions on display in Athens. But the fact is that God is in charge and we have neighbours of many faiths and ethnic backgrounds, first, second, third generation immigrant, British, refugee, asylum seeker. What is going on? What is this all about? We used to export our culture and the Christian faith to the rest of the world. Are the chickens coming home to roost?

Back to our memory and our future. God knows what he is doing. I don't know what his specific plans are for our country;

you'll have to buy a different kind of book from a different kind of author for that one. But I do know his plans are good. I suspect, though, that as we live a more distinctly welcoming faith, we'll be getting in on the act of what God has been doing bringing all this wonderful diversity to our doorstep.

Our age is one of contested space. Space to dress this way, worship that way. Express that freely, as long as you don't offend others or infringe on that space; live with whom you please, how you please, as long as people aren't affected by it. Space to be different together or, more likely, indifferent apart. Parallel communities exist the length and breadth of Britain. There are ethnic and religious groups living out the multicultural model, contributing to British life but barely making any contact with each other. The good news of the Christian faith demands more than merely tolerance. I don't want people to tolerate me! That suggests distance and coldness. I want to be accepted for who I am, not just tolerated! The God of incarnation, of relationship and boundary-crossing, calls us to reconciliation. Reconciliation requires acceptance of each other and knowledge of what we like and dislike about each other. I wonder if the challenge the church faces now is an opportunity for us to be the Christians God has always intended us to be: risky, vulnerable, loving, serving boundary-crossers! Distinctive yet welcoming.

Watch this space!

To continue this conversation, go to www.distinctlywelcoming.com